Advanced Mexican Spanish

Learn to Speak Like a Local in Mexico and Master Nuances and Slang with Ease

Free Bonuses from Cecilia Melero

Hi Spanish Learners!

My name is Cecilia Melero, and first off, I want to THANK YOU for reading my book.

Now you have a chance to join my exclusive Spanish language learning email list so you can get the ebooks below for free as well as the potential to get more Spanish books for free! Simply click the link below to join.

P.S. Remember that it's 100% free to join the list.

Access your free bonuses here:

https://livetolearn.lpages.co/advanced-mexican-spanish-paperback/

Or, Scan the QR code!

Table of Contents

Introduction

¡Hola, amigo! Welcome to *Advanced Mexican Spanish: Learn to Speak Like a Local in Mexico and Master Nuances and Slang with Ease.* If you've reached for this book, chances are you've already delved into *Mexican Spanish for Beginners: Your Guide to Speaking and Understanding the Language and Culture of Mexico with Confidence* and *Intermediate Mexican Spanish: The Ultimate Guide to Building Fluency and Cultural Insight for Everyday Conversations.*

However, whether you've followed our series or learned your Spanish skills in some other way – such as college courses, Latino friends, or family members with Mexican roots – your journey has led you here for a reason – your desire to finally become fluent in Mexican Spanish, and *Advanced Mexican Spanish: Learn to Speak Like a Local in Mexico and Master Nuances and Slang with Ease* is your comprehensive guide to achieving that goal and beyond!

For those who haven't read the previous books, our Mexican Spanish series follows George Donovan, a laid-back guy from the U.S., and Paula Solís, his Mexican friend, who happens to be a Spanish teacher! In the first book, George visits Paula in her hometown, Mexico City, and he takes the opportunity to learn all the basics of Spanish. In the second book, the duo met in Cancún and traveled through la Riviera Maya. After a week, George returned home as an intermediate Spanish student!

Now, the two friends have another adventure in mind: they will explore the central region of Mexico: Guanajuato, Querétaro, and San

Miguel de Allende. But, of course, in addition to road trips, they have another goal - to turn George into an advanced Mexican Spanish speaker!

After this 7-day trip to Mexico, George - and you - will become fluent in Spanish. First, you will review some important things you already know, like the Spanish pronunciation, pronouns and the main characteristics of verbs. Then, day by day, Paula will introduce new advanced topics, such as:

- Prefixes and suffixes
- Relative pronouns and adverbs
- Non-finite verb forms
- The conditional and he subjunctive
- The direct and indirect objects
- Impersonal constructions
- Active and passive voice
- Direct and indirect speech
- Reflexive verbs and pronouns
- Difficult Spanish words

But this is not all! Get ready to learn some reading comprehension strategies that will help you navigate all kinds of reading situations, and the writing tips will help you become as fluent in writing as you will become in speaking!

The book offers everyday examples, along with sections on vocabulary, useful phrases, and insights into Mexican culture. In addition, each chapter concludes with a comprehensive summary and an exercise section to test how much you've learned. At the end of the book, you'll find the answer key, where you can check your answers.

Once you finish *Advanced Mexican Spanish: Learn to Speak Like a Local in Mexico and Master Nuances and Slang with Ease*, you will have gone from an intermediate student to a fluent Mexican Spanish speaker. You'll be able to navigate complex situations, you'll understand what people say on TV, you'll be able to read a newspaper, and you will express complex ideas, feelings, and expectations clearly.

What are you waiting for? Turn the page and begin this journey to master Mexican Spanish right now! *¡Vamos! George y Paula te están esperando.*

0. Before We Begin

"*Señor,*" the flight attendant said as she gently touched my shoulder, "*vamos a aterrizar pronto. Por favor, ponga su asiento en posición vertical.*"

"*Sí, perdón,*" I replied with confusion, for I hadn't noticed my seat wasn't vertical in the first place.

The same flight attendant walked through the plane hall and asked everyone to fasten their seatbelts, even though the sign was on. The plane was about to take off, and with it, my Mexican adventure. This was my third trip to Mexico, and this time, Paula and I would meet in Guanajuato, a city in the center of the country known for its colonial architecture and rich mining history. I had about three and a half hours of clear-blue sky ahead of me, so I had to pass the time somehow...

Revision of Pronunciation

As the plane took to the skies, I had flashbacks of my two previous trips to Mexico. I remembered that first time . . . reading Paula's PDF printout on Spanish pronunciation and having a hard time understanding it. Now, already on my third trip and considering myself an almost advanced student, I decided to brush up on Mexican Spanish pronunciation without help. I took out a pen and the notebook I had bought for this third trip and made the following charts with the examples that came to mind. I started with the vowel sounds:

Vowel	Sounds like English...	Example	Pronunciation
A	ah	arrogancia	ah-rroh-<u>gahn</u>-see-ah
E	eh	empatía	ehm-pah-<u>tee</u>-ah
I	ee	historia	ees-<u>toh</u>-ree-ah
O	oh	opinión	oh-pee-<u>nee-ohn</u>
U	oo	cultura	kool-<u>too</u>-rah

I was proud of my chart. Paula's first chart had really short and simple words, but now I could come up with longer and more complex examples. I was about to move on to consonants but remembered the exceptions! When UE and UI follow G or Q, the U is silent:

Letters	Sounds like English...	Example	Pronunciation
GUE	geh	alber**gue**	ahl-<u>bher</u>-geh
GUI	gee	**gui**onista	geeoh-<u>nees</u>-tah
QUE	keh	ban**que**ro	bahn-<u>keh</u>-roh
QUI	kee	monar**quí**a	moh-nahr-<u>kee</u>-ah

And luckily, I also remembered the exception to the exception: when the U has diaeresis, that is, when we see these combinations: GÜE or GÜI, that U is *not silent.*

Letters	Sounds like English...	Example	Pronunciation
GÜE	gooeh	bilingüe	bee-leen-<u>gooeh</u>
GÜI	gooee	lingüística	leen-<u>gooees</u>-tee-kah

Now, yes, it was time to make my own chart with the consonant sounds:

Consonant	Sounds like English...	Example	Pronunciation
B, V	b	biodiversidad	beeoh-dee-behr-see-<u>dahd</u>
C, Q, K	k	riqueza escasez kilómetro	rree-<u>keh</u>-sah ehs-kah-<u>sehs</u> kee-<u>loh</u>-meh-troh
C, S, X	s	astucia xilofón	ahs-<u>too</u>-see-a see-loh-<u>fohn</u>
CH	ch	dicha	<u>dee</u>-chah
D	d	solidaridad	soh-lee-dah-ree-<u>dahd</u>
F	f	fanfarrón	fahn-fah-<u>rrohn</u>
G	g	abogada	ah-boh-<u>gah</u>-dah
G, J, X	h	generosidad juventud México	heh-neh-roh-see-<u>dahd</u> hoo-ben-<u>tood</u> <u>meh</u>-hee-koh

H	silent	honradez	ohn-<u>rrah</u>-dehs
L	l	valentía	bah-lehn-<u>tee</u>-ah
LL	y, j	llanura	yah-<u>noo</u>-rah
M	m	ambición	ahm-bee-<u>seeohn</u>
N	n	nostalgia	nohs-<u>tahl</u>-hee-ah
Ñ	ny	niñez	nee-<u>nyehs</u>
P	p	popularidad	poh-poo-lah-ree-<u>dahd</u>
R	tt, r	amargura	ah-mahr-<u>goo</u>-rah
R RR	rr	rencor derrota	rrehn-<u>kohr</u> deh-<u>rroh</u>-tah
T	t	sustantivo	soos-tahn-<u>tee</u>-boh
W	w	sándwich	<u>sahn</u>-weech
X	x s h	éxito xenofobia Oaxaca	<u>eh</u>-xee-toh seh-noh-<u>foh</u>-bee-ah wah-<u>hah</u>-kah
Y	y, j ee	yeísmo ley	yeh-<u>ees</u>-moh leh-ee

    I was so happy to be able to come up with an example for each of the pronunciations of the Spanish letters. There was only one thing I needed to review: I had learned that the Spanish letter R has two possible pronunciations. The soft pronunciation is a sound like the TT for "butter," and is used when the R is in the middle or at the end of a word.

The strong pronunciation is used when the R is the first letter of a word or when it's doubled. However, I learned that there is another case in which the strong R is used: when a letter R is preceded by D, L, N, S, or B. For example, the word *honrado* ("honest") is pronounced with a strong R: ohn-<u>rrah</u>-doh.

Revision of Personal and Possessive Pronouns

After making my pronunciation charts, I decided to review another subject I knew I needed to know by heart if I wanted to continue learning Spanish: pronouns. These words play a fundamental role in language, replacing or referring to a noun or group of nouns. They help us avoid repetition, express possession, and understand relationships.

Personal Pronouns

I started with personal pronouns, and I made a table I could go back to during my trip if I had any doubts:

Persona		Sujeto	Objeto directo	Objeto indirecto	Preposici onal
Singular	Primera	yo	me	me	mí
	Segunda	tú	te	te	ti
		usted	lo, la	le, se*	usted
	Tercera	él, ella	lo, la	le, se*	él, ella
Plural	Primera	nosotros, nosotras	nos	nos	nosotros, nosotras
	Segunda	ustedes	los, las	les, se*	ustedes
	Tercera	ellos, ellas	los, las	les, se*	ellos, ellas

* *Se* is used as an indirect object pronoun when we already have a direct object pronoun in the sentence. Let's check it with an example:

- *Escribí una carta a mi madre* ("I wrote a letter to my mother").

If I wanted to replace the direct object (*una carta*) with a pronoun, I'd get:

- *La escribí a mi madre* ("I wrote it to my mother").

On the other hand, if I wanted to replace the indirect object (*a mi madre*) with a pronoun, I'd get:

- *Le escribí una carta* ("I wrote a letter to her").

And what would happen if I wanted to replace both objects with pronouns? Saying *Le la escribí* sounds cacophonic and repetitive, that's why we replace the *le* with a *se*:

- *Se la escribí* ("I wrote it to her").

Possessive Adjectives

Now, it was time for possessives. I remembered from my first trip that possessive adjectives go before the noun and are used to show that a thing belongs to somebody or that a person is related to somebody. They are adjectives, so they agree in number and gender (only in some cases) with the person or object that is possessed. This is the chart of possessive adjectives:

Persona que posee	*Persona o cosa poseída*	
	Singular	*Plural*
yo	*mi*	*mis*
tú	*tu*	*tus*
usted	*su*	*sus*
él, ella	*su*	*sus*
nosotros	*nuestro* * *nuestra* * *	*nuestros* * *nuestras* * *

ustedes	su	sus
ellos, ellas	su	sus

* *Si la persona o cosa poseída es masculina.*
** *Si la persona o cosa poseída es femenina.*

Possessive adjectives are pretty easy; the only thing to remember is that the adjectives agree in number (and in gender only for *nuestro, nuestra, nuestros,* and *nuestras*) with the thing or person possessed.

Possessive Pronouns

As with all pronouns, possessive pronouns take the place of nouns. And, as their name indicates, we use them to show possession. To choose the correct pronouns, you have to look at the gender and number of the thing possessed AND the person and number of the possessor. This is the chart I made on the plane:

Persona que posee	Cosa poseída			
	Singular (una cosa)		Plural (más de una cosa)	
	Femenina	Masculina	Femenina	Masculina
yo	mía	mío	mías	míos
tú	tuya	tuyo	tuyas	tuyos
usted	suya	suyo	suyas	suyos
él, ella	suya	suyo	suyas	suyos
nosotros, nosotras	nuestra	nuestro	nuestras	nuestros
ustedes	suya	suyo	suyas	suyos
ellos, ellas	suya	suyo	suyas	suyos

And with that chart, I finished reviewing personal and possessive pronouns.

Revision of Properties of Verbs

Verbs were the last important subject I wanted to review before landing in Mexico and starting my third learning trip. However, I didn't think studying lists of verbs and conjugations would be helpful. I wanted to really understand and incorporate the properties of verbs. So, I took out all the notes I had on verbs, and I made a recap of the basic features of verbs:

- number
- person
- voice
- mood
- tense

Spanish verbs are a bit more complex than in English. The verb contains a lot of information. So, to really master Spanish verbs, Paula had told me that I needed to study their properties and their importance in conjugation.

I started reviewing the three conjugations. Spanish verbs are divided into three groups (also called *conjugations*) according to their infinitive ending, and the regular verbs of each of these groups behave in the same way when we conjugate them. The first group is made of the verbs that end in *-ar*. In the second group, we have the verbs ending in *-er*. The third conjugation has the verbs ending in *-ir*.

Another essential thing to remember is the *morphology* of verbs, that is, their internal structure. Verbs have a stem or root and an ending. The stem contains the semantic information – the meaning of the verb. In regular verbs, the root never changes, which is great! It's the part of the verb that comes before the *-ar, -er,* or *-ir* ending.

On the other hand, these endings change according to number, person, voice, mood, and tense. Luckily, in regular verbs, they change according to a pattern and according to the three conjugations I mentioned before.

All this will become clearer with an example. Let's take the verb *cantar* ("to sing"). Since it ends in *-ar*, we can say that it belongs to the first conjugation. Then, we can say that *cant-* is the root and that, since it's a regular verb, it will stay the same when we conjugate it: *Yo canto* ("I sing"), *tú cantabas* ("you sang"), *ella cantará* ("she will sing"), etc.

After this introduction, I will analyze each of the grammatical features that affect the verbs in Spanish.

Number

Verbs must agree in number with the subject of the sentence. In other words, verbs change if the subject is singular (one person or thing) or plural (more than one person or thing). For example:

• *Yo bailé mucho* ("I danced a lot").

• Nosotras bailamos mucho ("We danced a lot").

Person

Of course, verbs also agree in person, i.e., who is doing the action. There are three persons, and, in turn, each one has a singular and a plural option. I already knew this. I had even applied it to my previous charts, but I wanted to write it down *one more time.*

The first person is reflected in the pronouns *yo* ("I"), *nosotros,* and *nosotras* ("we"). The second person is reflected in the pronouns *usted, tú* ("you" singular) and *ustedes* ("you" plural). The third person is reflected in the pronouns *él* ("he"), *ella* ("she"), *ellos* and *ellas* ("they"). And now, let's see how a verb changes according to the person who performs the action:

• *Yo estudio español* ("I study Spanish").

• Nosotras estudiamos mucho ("We study a lot").

• *¿Ustedes estudian juntas?* ("Do you study together?").

• *Él no estudia Medicina* ("He doesn't study Medicine").

• *Mis primos estudian afuera* ("My cousins study abroad").

Voice

As in English, in Spanish, we have active and passive voices. Paula said this was one of the subjects she would explain on my trip, but I was intrigued and did some research beforehand. I learned that we choose between passive and active voice depending on whether we want to emphasize a sentence's subject or object. We normally use the active voice. To form the passive, we split the verb into two: the verb *ser* conjugated in the same tense as the sentence in active voice + the participle of the main verb.

Let's look at an example. First, we'll see a sentence in active voice, and then we'll transform it into the passive voice:

- Los legisladores **aprobaron** la ley ("Lawmakers passed the law").

- La ley **fue aprobada** por los legisladores ("The law was passed by lawmakers").

Here, my research ended because I knew Paula would explain it to me on the trip!

Mood

Mood is a feature of verbs that indicates the speaker's attitude toward what they are saying. This, in turn, reflects the intention of the sentence. Spanish has three moods: indicative, subjunctive, and imperative.

The indicative is used to talk about things that are true or certain. We used the subjunctive mood to refer to wishes, doubts, and possibilities. Lastly, the imperative is used to give commands or orders.

Now, we'll see three examples that came up during my flight, one in each of the three moods:

- Indicative: *Es la hora de la cena* ("It's dinner time").

- Subjunctive: *Ojala haya una opción vegetariana* ("I hope there's a vegetarian option").

- Imperative: *Tráigame la pasta, por favor* ("Bring me the pasta dish, please").

Tense

Tense was the last feature of verbs that I needed to review. It's a feature that expresses a time reference – mainly past, present, and future. I already knew quite a few Spanish tenses, so I decided to make a chart describing when to use each one:

Tiempo verbal	Usos	Ejemplo
Presente simple	Habits and regular actions Timetables Instructions and recipes Universal truths Storytelling	*Juego al fútbol los lunes* ("I play soccer on Mondays"). *El avión aterriza a las 10* ("The plane lands at 10"). *El Sol sale por el este* ("The Sun rises in the east").
Presente continuo	Things that are happening at the moment of speaking Ongoing actions	*Estoy yendo a México* ("I'm going to Mexico"). *Estoy entrenando para una maratón* ("I'm training for a marathon").
Pretérito imperfecto	Past actions, habits, or routines	*De niño, cantaba en un coro* ("As a child, I used to sing in a choir").
Pretérito perfecto simple	Actions that started and finished in the past	*Hice la valija ayer* ("I made my bags yesterday").
Pretérito pluscuamperfecto	Actions that happened before another past action	*El día anterior, había lavado la ropa que quería traer* ("The day before, I had washed the clothes I wanted to bring").
Futuro simple	Future actions	*Seré un estudiante avanzado de español* ("I'll be an advanced Spanish student").

Tiempo verbal	Usos	Ejemplo
Futuro perifrástico	Closer future actions	*Apenas aterrice, me voy a comer un taco* ("As soon as I land, I'm going to have a taco").
Condicional simple	Wishes, obligations, suggestions, polite requests, speculations	*Me gustaría ver una película* ("I'd like to watch a movie").

Having reviewed the Spanish pronunciation, the personal and possessive pronouns, and the features of the Spanish verbs, it was time to watch a movie and relax for the rest of the flight.

1. *Lunes: Nuevas aventuras, nuevas estructuras*

After an educational flight, my plane landed in Aeropuerto Internacional de Guanajuato – just as the sun was rising. This time, Paula picked me up in her car with a sign that said "George." I ran up to her as soon as I saw her, and we hugged each other intensely. It had been a year since we had seen each other's faces after we had gone our separate ways in Cancun.

"*¡Hola, George!*" said Paula. "*¿Cómo estás? ¿Listo para aprender más español?*"

"*¡Claro que sí!*" I replied with a big smile.

I had been studying a lot back home, but this trip was my chance to really consolidate my Spanish knowledge with more advanced topics, and what better way to do it than learning from the best native teacher ever?

Prefixes and Suffixes

Before Paula took me to our hotel, we decided to grab a coffee at the airport and have a quick lesson. I had forgotten how delicious Mexican coffee is compared to the kind we get in the US!

The topic of this learning session was prefixes and suffixes.

Prefixes

According to Paula, prefixes comprise one letter or a group of letters that constitute a unit of meaning, and they are placed before another word or group of letters to form a different meaning. They can be categorized according to their meanings. My friend explained each category by providing lists and gave me key examples for each of them.

Prefixes of Place

- *intra-:* intramuscular ("intramuscular"), intravenoso ("intravenous")
- *endo-:* endoesqueleto ("endoskeleton"), endogamia ("endogamy")
- *exo-:* exoesqueleto ("exoesqueleto"), exótico ("exotic")
- *extra-:* extraterrestre ("extraterrestrial"), extraordinario ("extraordinary")
- *infra-:* inframundo ("underworld"), infrahumano ("subhuman")
- *sub-:* subacuático ("underwater"), submarino ("submarine")
- *sobre-:* sobresaliente ("outstanding")
- *super-/supra-:* suprasensible ("suprasensitive"), superponer ("to overlay")
- *entre-:* entrepierna ("crotch")
- *inter-:* intermedio ("intermediate"), intercalar ("intersperse")
- *retro-:* retrovisor ("rearview mirror")
- *ante-:* antebrazo ("forearm"), anteojos ("glasses")
- *trans-/tras-:* transbordador ("shuttle"), trasfondo ("background")
- *a-/ad-:* adjuntar ("to attach"), adyacente ("adjacent")

Prefixes of Time

- *ante-:* anterior ("previous"), antepasados ("ancestors")
- *ex-:* expresidente ("former president"), exnovio ("ex-boyfriend")
- *pos-/post-:* posponer ("to postpone"), posteridad ("posterity")
- *pre-:* predecir ("to predict"), preaviso ("notice")
- *trans-/tras-:* transformar ("to transform"), transcribir ("to transcribe")

Prefixes of Quantity
- **multi-:** *multicultural* ("multicultural"), *multifacético* ("multifaceted")
- **pluri-:** *plurinacional* ("plurinational"), *pluridimensional* ("multidimensional")
- **poli-:** *poliamor* ("polyamory"), *políglota* ("polyglot")
- **mono-:** *monogamia* ("monogamy"), *monoteísmo* ("monotheism")
- **bi-:** *bisexual* ("bisexual"), *bicicleta* ("bicycle")
- **tri-:** *triciclo* ("tricycle"), *tridente* ("trident")
- **mili-:** *milímetro* ("millimeter")

Prefixes of Gradation or Intensity
- **re-:** *releer* ("to reread"), *reelegir* ("to reelect")
- **super-:** *superhéroe* ("superhero"), *superpotencia* ("superpower")
- **archi-:** *archienemigo* ("archenemy"), *archiduque* ("archduke")
- **hiper-:** *hipertiroidismo* ("hyperthyroidism"), *hipertensión* ("hypertension")
- **entre-:** *entrecerrar* ("to squint")
- **vice-:** *viceministro/a* ("vice-minister"), *vicepresidente/a* ("vice-president")

Negative Prefixes
- **im-/in-:** *imposible* ("impossible"), *ineficiente* ("inefficient")
- **des-:** *desarmar* ("to disarm"), *desobedecer* ("disobey")
- **dis-:** *discordia* ("discord"), *disconforme* ("dissatisfied")
- **a-:** *ahistórico* ("ahistorical")
- **des-:** *desaprobar* ("to disapprove"), *desenchufar* ("to unplug")
- **an-:** *anarquista* ("anarchist")

Prefixes of Orientation or Disposition
- **anti-:** *antisistema* ("anti-system"), *anticlimático* ("anticlimactic")
- **contra-:** *contraataque* ("counterattack")
- **pro-:** *proindependentista* ("pro-independence")

Suffixes

While we were waiting for the check, we saw how suffixes work. In many languages, speakers find links between certain word families, like the one we see in "defend," "defender," "defense," and "defensive." Depending on how they end (that is, depending on their *suffixes*), we can understand whether we are talking about a verb, a noun, or an adjective. In some cases, I realized that some suffixes also required a couple extra tweaks, like adding an extra letter (e.g., *noche* → *anoche<u>cer</u>*). These are the suffixes Paula taught me, and together, we came up with some example words for each of them:

Suffixes to Make Verbs

- **-ear:** *broma* → *bromear* ("to make jokes"), *hoja* → *hojear* ("to skim through")
- **-cer/-ecer:** *noche* → *anochecer* ("to get dark"), *flor* → *florecer* ("to bloom")
- **-ificar:** *edificio* → *edificar* ("to build"), identidad → *identificar* *("to identify")*
- **-izar:** *agudo/a* → *agudizar* ("to sharpen"), *impermeable* → *impermeabilizar* ("to waterproof")

Suffixes to Make Adjectives

- **-able:** transporte → transportable ("transportable"), colección → coleccionable ("collectible")
- **-áceo/a:** violeta → violáceo/a ("purplish"), gris → grisáceo ("grayish")
- **-aco/a:** Polonia → polaco/a ("Polish"), manía → maníaco/a ("manic")
- **-al:** verbo → verbal ("verbal"), norma → normal ("normal")
- **-áneo/a:** instante → instantáneo/a ("instantaneous"), cutis → cutáneo ("cutaneous")
- **-ante:** delirio → delirante ("delusional")
- **-ario/a:** banco → bancario/a ("banking"), planeta → planetario/a ("planetary")
- **-ente/-iente:** calor → caliente ("hot")
- **-ento/a:** atención → atento/a ("attentive")

- **-érrimo/a:** pobre → paupérrimo/a ("very poor"), acre → acérrimo/a ("staunch")
- **-ible:** horror → horrible ("horrible"),
- **-ico/a:** historia → histórico/a ("historical"), escultura → escultórico/a ("sculptural")
- **ifico/a:** honor → honorífico/a ("honorary"), paz → pacífico/a ("peaceful")
- **-il:** joven → juvenil ("juvenile"), infante → infantil ("infantile")
- **-ino/a:** can → canino/a ("canine")
- **-ísimo/a:** bello/a → bellísimo/a ("very beautiful"), duro → durísimo ("very hard")
- **-ivo/a:** esquivar → esquivo/a ("elusive")
- **-izo/a:** mover → movedizo/a ("shifting"), correr → corredizo/a ("sliding")
- **-oso/a:** peligro → peligroso/a ("dangerous")

Suffixes to Make Nouns

Professions or social roles

- **-dor/-dora:** trabajo → trabajador/a ("worker"), maquillaje → maquillador/a ("makeup stylist")
- **-dero/a:** pan → panadero/a ("baker")
- **-ero/a:** jardín → jardinero/a ("gardener"), ingeniería → ingeniero/a ("engineer")
- **-ista:** economía → economista ("economist"), malabares → malabarista ("juggler")

Groups and objects

- *-ero:* ceniza → cenicero ("ashtray")
- *-ado:* alumnos → alumnado ("student body"),
- *-ario:* vecino → vecindario ("neighborhood")
- *-ía:* ciudadano → ciudadanía ("citizenship")
- *-ería:* cerveza → cervecería ("pub")

Nouns that come from verbs

- **-ada:** apuñalar → puñalada ("stabbing"), abofetear → bofetada ("slap")

- **-aje:** aterrizar → aterrizaje ("landing"), sabotear → sabotaje ("sabotage")

- **-ción:** grabar → grabación ("recording"), actuar → acción ("action")

- **-ducción:** deducir → deducción ("deduction"), conducir → conducción ("conduction")

- **-ección:** corregir → corrección ("correction"), elegir → elección ("election")

- **-epción:** recibir → recepción ("reception"), concebir → concepción ("conception")

- **-dura:** quemar → quemadura ("burn"), lastimar → lastimadura ("injure")

- **-ido:** ladrar → ladrido ("bark"), sonar → sonido ("sound")

- **ión:** expresar → expresión ("expression"), reunir → reunión ("reunion")

- **-miento:** crecer → crecimiento ("growth"), casar → casamiento ("marriage")

- **-ncia:** tender → tendencia ("tendency"), discrepar → discrepancia ("discrepancy")

- **-ón:** empujar → empujón ("push"), aventar → aventón ("lift")

- **-scripción:** inscribir → inscripción ("inscription"), describir → descripción ("description")

- **-sición:** posicionar → posición ("position"), componer → composición ("composition")

- **-sión:** divertirse → diversión ("fun"), imprimir → impresión ("printout")

Nouns that come from adjectives

- **-dad/-tad:** leal → lealtad ("loyalty"), humilde → humildad ("humility")

- **-bilidad:** estable → estabilidad ("stability"), amable → amabilidad ("kindness")

- **-edad:** nuevo/a → novedad ("novelty"), breve → brevedad ("brevity")

- **-era:** borracho/a → borrachera ("binge"), ciego/a → ceguera ("blindness")
- **-ería:** tonto/a → tontería ("foolishness"), pedante → pedantería ("pedantry")
- **-ez:** viejo/a → vejez ("old age"), rígido/a → rigidez ("stiffness")
- **-eza:** grande → grandeza ("greatness"), perezoso/a → pereza ("laziness")
- **-ía:** alegre → alegría ("joy"), cercano/a → cercanía ("closeness")
- **-idad:** feliz → felicidad ("happiness"), irregular → irregularidad ("irregularity")
- **-ismo:** vegano/a → veganismo ("veganism"), social → socialismo ("socialism")
- **-ncia:** vago → vagancia ("laziness"), permanente → permanencia ("permanence")
- **-ura:** caliente → calentura ("fever"), amargo/a → amargura ("bitterness")

After paying for our coffees, we got into Paula's car and headed to our hotel. When we arrived, I had to check in at the front desk. It was a lovely colonial mansion in the middle of the city, so I could already enjoy the incredible architecture that makes this city famous among tourists. After getting to our rooms and unpacking, it was time to explore the historic center.

Our first stop was the *Alhóndiga de Granaditas*, an eighteenth-century building built during an era of viceroyalty. As we learned during the guided tour, it is known for its key role in Mexican independence. However, in 1958, the *Alhóndiga* became the Regional Museum of Guanajuato.

Infinitives, Participles, and Gerunds

As we walked through this amazing building, Paula continued with the Spanish lessons, giving me a grammatical definition of infinitives:

"Infinitives," she said, "are a non-personal form of verbs that, together with participles and gerunds, make up a type of word called **nonfinite verb** (*verboide* in Spanish). A non-personal form means I cannot use this verboide as a normal verb; I cannot think of a subject of that action and put together an ordinary sentence.

Then, she wrote some notes in a little notebook:

Personal form of the verb *comer: El niño come queso*

- *el niño* = subject (person)
- *come* = conjugated verb, with the same person and number as the subject
- *queso* = DO

Incorrect sentences using *verboides*:

- X El niño **comer** queso (infinitivo)
- X El niño **comido** queso (participio)
- X El niño **comiendo** queso (gerundio)

When we left the museum, we decided to visit the *Callejón del Beso* ("the Kiss Alley"), a very narrow street made up of two houses painted in red and orange. These homes have balconies less than a meter apart, making it possible to talk to someone from terrace to terrace – or even kiss!

Infinitives

Then, as we shared a *refresco* under the balconies, I asked Paula to explain infinitives one more time:

"Basically, an infinitive is a non-personal form of a verb," she said.

"I know you already explained this concept, but could you talk to me like if I were a 5-year-old, please?" I replied.

"A non-personal form of a verb," said Paula, "means that this word carries an action meaning, like 'to eat,' but it is a word that isn't linked to any particular subject. That's why we call them 'non-personal forms', because we need to assign this infinitive a subject in order to use it, and that's when this *verboide* becomes an actual verb."

According to Paula, we can find infinitives in different grammar contexts. First, we can spot them in compound verbs (an action that uses more than one action word), typically with a modal verb:

- Yo quiero **comer** sano
- Ellos pueden **bailar** salsa
- Los niños deben **ir** a la escuela

Then, infinitives can also function as the subject of a sentence. We can say this is the case when we can replace this word with a noun or with the words *esto/a/os/as* ("this"), just like:

- **Pescar** es un gran pasatiempo → **La pesca/Esto** es un gran pasatiempo

- **Fumar** es malo para la salud → **Los cigarrillos/Estos** son malos para la salud

- Me encanta **cantar** → Me encanta **el canto/esto**

Paula also reminded me that sometimes an infinitive may be united to a pronoun at the end, forming a single word. This grammatical phenomenon is called *pronombre enclítico,* and it's something that English doesn't have. For example:

- Me gusta la música electrónica. Me gusta escuchar**la**

- Amar**te** es lo único que sé hacer

- Estoy enojada con Juan pero no quiero decír**selo**

I noticed that the pronouns that could be added corresponded both to a direct object and an indirect one. Sometimes, when we have a verbal periphrasis (Paula told me she would explain this in just a minute, but it's basically when we have two verbs that work together to form a new meaning), we can either place the pronoun next to the infinitive or write it separately, but not both at the same time. The pronouns need to stick together:

- *La quiero ver = Quiero ver**la*** ("I want to see her")

- *Los estuvimos llamando por horas = Estuvimos llamándo**los** por horas* ("We were calling you for hours")

- *¿Se lo puedes decir mañana? = ¿Podrás decír**selo** mañana?* ("Can you tell him tomorrow?")

Participles

Then, we walked towards a massive property cataloged as a national heritage site, with tall yellow walls and beautiful details. Outside this stunning facade, Paula explained how *participios* work:

"Participles carry that name because a participle **participates** within the sentence both as a **verb** and as an **adjective**. Participles act like verbs because sometimes they can have an active meaning, such as *amante* ('lover'), and sometimes they can be passive, like in *amado/a* ('loved'). Then, they act like adjectives because they can be used to modify nouns: *el perro amado* ('the beloved dog'). The regular passive participle ends in **-ado** in verbs of the first conjugation and in **-ido** in verbs of the second and third conjugations."

As far as I understood, as a general rule, participles are formed by adding **-ado/-ada/-ados/-ados/-adas** or **-ido/-ida/-idos/-idos/-idas** to the root of the verb, but this only happens when we use this word to describe a noun, like in *el amado perro*:

- Amar → Am/ar → Am + ado → Amado → Amado/a/os/as: La mujer amada.
- Comer → Com/er → Com + ido → Comido → Comido/a/os/as: Los chocolates comidos.
- Vivir→ Vivir → Viv/ir → Viv + ido → Vivido → Vivido/a/os/as: Los años vividos.

However, when we use participles as part of a compound verb form, like in the *pretérito pluscuamperfecto* tense, we don't see a variation of gender or number:

- Yo había **amado**
- Ella había **amado**
- Ustedes habíamos **amado**

Then, I remembered that there were some irregular participles to keep in mind, such as in *Yo había muerto* ("I had died"). Thankfully, Paula gave me a chart with more common irregular participles:

Infinitivo	Participio	Infinitivo	Participio
volver	*vuelto*	*abrir*	*abierto*
ver	*visto*	*cubrir*	*cubierto*
morir	*muerto*	*decir*	*dicho*
poner	*puesto*	*predecir*	*predicho*
hacer	*hecho*	*escribir*	*escrito*
imprimir	*impreso*	*resolver*	*resuelto*

Gerunds

Finally, we went to the Casa de las artesanías de Guanajuato, with objects known for its beautiful craftsmanship and originality. While we observed every detail, it was time we revised *gerundios*.

I noticed I already used gerunds when using the *presente continuo*, with the verb *estar*: *Yo estoy hablando contigo, Yo estoy aprendiendo español*. This means that gerunds are a type of word that can be used in compound verbs and that they can end either in **-ando** or **-endo**.

Of course there are irregular gerunds to take into consideration, as this chart Paula gave me showed:

Tipo de irregularidad	*Ejemplo*
Verbs with a root ending in a vowel → Swap the I in *-iendo* for a **Y**	*huyendo (huir)* *leyendo (leer)* *yendo (ir)*
Verbs with a root ending in an Ñ → The **Ñ** remains	*gruñendo (gruñir)*
Second and third conjugation verbs with a vowel change (O to UE) → Swap an O for an **U**	*muriendo (morir → él muere)* *pudiendo (poder → él puede)* *durmiendo (dormir → él duerme)*
Third conjugation verbs that feature a change of vowels (E to IE or I) in the present tense → Swap an E for an **I**	*diciendo (decir → él dice)* *viniendo (venir → él viene)* *mintiendo (mentir → él miente)*

"If Infinitives can function as nouns and participles can function as adjectives, what about the gerunds?" I asked Paula after she had finished her explanation.

"Good question," said Paula. "Well, gerunds can be found as adverbs in specific contexts, like in *Ella vino corriendo* ('She came running'), which would be the same as to say *Ella vino rápidamente*."

After a long afternoon, I wanted to go back to the hotel to take a shower and, most of all, a nap!

Verbal Periphrasis to Mark Time Perspective

After a great shower and some restful sleep, I was ready to go out again. Paula suggested we go to a local eatery to enjoy some local cuisine. There was a lovely restaurant that was known for its *enchiladas mineras*, a traditional Mexican dish with a special filling of cheese, onions, carrots and potatoes, all mixed into a kind of stew. While we waited for our meal, I told Paula that she could teach me one more topic for the day, so she chose to talk about verbal paraphrases

Now, *verboides* are extremely helpful when it comes to adding nuances to our verbs. This happens when we use *perífrasis verbales* or verbal periphrasis. These are two verbs that, when used together, acquire a whole new meaning. In general, the structure includes an auxiliary verb (conjugated), plus a preposition and the main verb, which can be either an infinitive, a participle or a gerund.

"But how can I know which *verboide* to use?!" I asked Paula with unease.

"Don't worry!" she replied. "It's not that difficult. In fact, you already know that modal verbs take the infinitive as the main verb, as in *Debo despertarme temprano* ('I have to get up early') or in *Este anillo tiene que ser de Ana* ('This ring must be Ana's'). You also know how to use the *futuro perifrástico* in sentences like *Yo voy a ir al cine mañana*. However, let me give you a couple of tables with some key *perífrasis* about time!"

As usual, Paula had everything covered: she took three laminated tables out of her purse and handed them over to me.

Verbal Periphrasis with Infinitives

This is what the first chart looked like:

Perífrasis verbales con infinitivos		
Perífrasis verbal	*Inglés*	*Ejemplo*
estar por + inf	"about to"	*Estamos por comer* ("We are about to eat")
estar a punto de + inf		*Mi hijo está a punto de llegar* ("Mi son is about to arrive")
acabar de + inf	"just"	*Mi clase acaba de terminar* ("Mi class just ended")
comenzar a + inf	beginning	*¿El metro ya comenzó a funcionar?* ("Has the metro already started working?")
empezar a + inf		*Empezamos a reírnos de su chiste* ("We started to laugh at his joke")
pasar a + inf		*Ahora, pasaré a tomar lista, alumnos* ("I will now take roll call, students")
echarse a + inf	sudden beginning	*Ella se echó a llorar* ("She burst into tears")
ponerse a + inf		*El forastero se puso a tocar la guitarra* ("The stranger began to play the guitar")
dar (a alguien) por + inf		*Ahora le dio por hacer danza árabe* ("Now he has taken to Arabian dance")

terminar de + inf	ending	*¿Terminaste de comer, querido?* ("Have you finished eating, dear?")
dejar de + inf	sudden ending	*¡Deja de molestarme!* ("Stop bugging me!")
parar de + inf		*El tren paró de moverse* ("The train stopped moving")
acabar por + inf	"end up," "even"	*Insistió tanto que acabé por decirle la verdad* ("He insisted so much that I ended up saying the truth")
terminar por + inf		*Terminé por anotarme en 6 cursos este año* ("I ended up enrolling in 6 courses this year.")
llegar a + inf		*Ella llegó a renunciar debido a su jefe* ("She even resigned because of her boss")
volver a + inf	"again"	*¿Volviste a ver la película?* ("Did you watch the film again?")
tardar en + inf	duration	*Tardamos media hora en llegar al teatro* ("It took us half an hour to get to the theater")
acostumbrarse a + inf	habit	*Todavía no me acostumbro a estar solo* ("I still can't get used to being alone")
soler + iinf		*Yo solía acampar mucho cuando era niño* ("I used to camp a lot when I was a kid ")

Verbal Periphrasis with Participles

The *enchiladas* arrived! I was so happy to taste Mexican flavors once again. Here's the second chart Paula gave me:

Perífrasis verbales con participios		
Perífrasis verbal	*Inglés*	*Ejemplo*
andar + part	feeling	*Ando algo molesto por este tema* ("I am a bit upset about this issue")
estar + part	result	*Este filete está quemado...* ("This steak is burnt...")
dejar + part		*El entrenamiento me dejó agotada* ("The training left me exhausted")
quedar + part		*¡Mi proyecto quedó arruinado!* ("My project is ruined!")
llevar + part	resulted amount	*Llevo ahorrados 1.000 dólares hasta ahora* ("I have saved $1,000 so far")
dar por + part	ending	*Ana da por concluido su viaje* ("Ana concludes her trip")
tener + part		*Tengo tatuada a mi madre en el brazo* ("I have my mom tattooed on my arm")

Verbal Periphrasis with Gerund

Finally, it was time to ask for the check. While we waited, Paula handed me another chart with other verb uses of the gerund other than the *presente continuo* tense:

Perífrasis verbales con gerundios		
Perífrasis verbal	*Inglés*	*Ejemplo*
seguir + ger	"keep"	*¿Sigues saliendo con Juan?* ("Are you still seeing Juan?")
continuar + ger		*Las naciones continuaron peleando hasta 1997* ("The nations continued fighting until 1997")
andar + ger	ongoing action (now)	*¿Qué andan haciendo tus hijos?* ("What are your children up to?")
llevar + ger	ongoing action (for a while)	*¡Llevo media hora esperándote!* ("I've been waiting for you for half an hour!")
venir + ger		*Venimos viéndonos hace 3 años* ("We have been seeing each other for 3 years")
ir + ger	progression	*Vamos yendo; Nico está esperándonos en el cine* ("Let's get going; Nico is waiting for us at the cinema")
pasar(se)	"spend"	*Ella pasa horas pintando su casa* ("She spends hours painting her house")

Mexican Cultural Annex

It had been a lovely evening. With both our bellies and our hearts filled with Mexican joy, we returned to our hotel. Before we went to bed, Paula thought it would be fun for me to learn some common Spanish expressions that use verbal paraphrases. These are very popular in all Spanish-speaking countries, not just in Mexico, so they would prove to be useful in many conversations:

- *Dar por sentado* ("take for granted")
  - *No des por sentados a tus padres* ("Don't take your parents for granted")
- *Dar por hecho* ("consider it done" or "be sure of that")
  - *Te acompañaré mañana, dalo por hecho* ("I will accompany you tomorrow, be sure of that")
- *Ir a parar* ("to end up")
  - *Su juguete favorito fue a parar a la basura* ("His favorite toy ended up in the garbage")
- *Echar a perder* ("to spoil")
  - *¡La leche se echa a perder muy rápido!* ("Milk spoils very quickly!")
- *Dar a conocer* ("to announce, to reveal")
  - *El rey dio a conocer el nombre de su primogénito* ("The king announced the name of his firstborn")
- *Dar a entender* ("to hint, to imply")
  - *Ella me dio a entender que le gustas* ("She hinted to me that she likes you")

Chapter Summary

Even though it had been a long day, I still wanted to revise what I learned with Paula:

- First of all, we learned a LONG list of Spanish prefixes and suffixes to make nouns, adjectives, and verbs, like the news featured in **bi**cicleta, hermo**sura,** and **trans**formación.
- Then, Paula taught me the theory behind the three *verboides* we have in Spanish: infinitives, participle, and gerunds, and we

saw which functions they can have within a sentence.

• Finally, we finished the lesson with different verbal paraphrases we could make using these *verboides*.

Exercises

1. Come up with one example for the six types of Spanish prefixes and for the three types of Spanish suffixes.

2. Complete the following chart with the missing *verboides*:

imprimir		
	amado	
		prediciendo
		yendo
mentir		
	leído	

3. Complete the following sentences using the infinitive, participle or gerund of the verbs in brackets:

    a. *Sigo _____ (buscar) mi teléfono; no sé dónde está.*

    b. *No te pongas esa camisa, está _____ (arrugar).*

    c. *El avión está a punto de _____ (despegar).*

    d. *Dieron por _____ (concluir) la reunión.*

    e. *Hemos pasado horas _____ (recorrer).*

4. Explain why infinitives, participles, and gerunds are non-personal forms of a verb.

5. Write six example sentences of verbal periphrasis: two using infinitives, two using participles, and two using gerunds.

2. *Martes: Si fuera tú...*

It was a beautiful Tuesday morning in Guanajuato, Mexico, and a day of adventures awaited us. I went to Paula's room to wake her up; we enjoyed a lovely continental breakfast at the hotel and headed to our first stop: the impressive Museo de las Momias! To get there, we crossed the *plaza de las ranas* (a square with a pool and frog sculptures on each corner).

Imperfecto progresivo

On our way to the museum, Paula thought it was time for me to learn two other verb tenses that require the use of *verboides*, these non-definite verbs because they would help me enrich my grammar skills. The first one was called the *imperfecto progresivo.*

According to my friend, the imperfect progressive is a compound verb tense that works like the *presente continuo* but for **ongoing past actions**. It is frequently used in conjunction with another action in the *pretérito perfecto simple* as a way of setting the scenario for that second action, as in these examples:

- **Estaba cocinando** *cuando sonó el timbre* ("I was cooking when the doorbell rang")

- *Ellas* **estaban caminando** *tranquilas hasta que un árbol cayó frente a ellas* ("They were walking quietly until a tree fell in front of them")

- *¿Qué **estabas haciendo** cuando te llamé?* ("What were you doing when I called you?")

In these examples, the action in the *pretérito perfecto simple* interrupts the action in the *imperfecto progresivo* and provokes a change. That's why we usually use the relative pronoun **cuando** to symbolize this moment.

"So, to form the *imperfecto progresivo*, all we have to do is conjugate the **auxiliary verb estar in the pretérito imperfecto** tense and add a **gerund** as the action verb, right?" I asked Paula.

"Yes, but that's not the only option," she replied. "You can also use verbs like *ir, seguir, venir, andar*, etc.."

Paula gave me some more examples with these words:

- ***Venía caminando*** *cuando de repente me caí* ("I was walking when I suddenly fell")
- *Maitena **iba leyendo** en el autobús cuando escuchó un ruido* ("Maitena was reading on the bus when she heard a noise")
- *Ellos **seguían escuchando** la clase cuando alguien abrió la puerta* ("They were still listening to the class when someone opened the door")

Pretérito perfecto compuesto

The museum was both eerie and fascinating: we were able to appreciate the mummified remains of Guanajuato's geographical and cultural ancestors from the seventeenth century, and it's the world's largest mummy collection!

After learning about the *imperfecto progresivo*, it was time to learn about the *pretérito perfecto compuesto*, which is similar to the *pretérito perfecto simple,* but this new tense holds many nuances of meaning that Paula introduced me to. In a way, it works like the present perfect does in English because it refers to actions or states that happened in the past, but their effects continue in the present.

For example, when I say *Aún no he visitado Madrid* ("I haven't visited Madrid yet"), this is a past action that still affects the moment of speech. This means that the *pretérito perfecto compuesto* is not focused on the past event itself but on its effect in the present. That's why it doesn't matter exactly when that action occurred. In another example, the sentence *Yo he probado comida vietnamita* ("I've tasted Vietnamese cuisine") refers to a past event (i.e., having tasted this food before), but that experience still affects you today.

To use this tense, we need the auxiliary verb *haber* in the present, plus a participle. I remembered this verb because of its impersonal version, **hay**, which we use to describe existence. However, in order to conjugate it in every person, I had to learn by heart a chart Paula gave me:

Sujeto	Verbo	Pretérito perfecto compuesto
Yo	**he**	Yo he amado
Tú	**has**	Tú has amado
Él/Ella/Usted	**ha**	Él/Ella ha amado
Nosotros/Nosotras	**hemos**	Nosotros/Nosotras hemos amado
Ustedes	**han**	Ustedes han amado
Ellos/Ellas	**han**	Ellos/Ellas han amado

As Paula told me, there are different contexts in which one should use the *pretérito perfecto compuesto*:

First of all, we use this tense to describe an experience, something that has taken place once or possibly many times in the past (as in *Yo he probado comida vietnamita*), or something that has not taken place, as in *Nunca he hablado con ella* ("I've never talked to her").

Secondly, we have an ongoing scenario that links actions to a limited time period that still continues today, as in *He dado mi vida por mi familia* ("I've given my life for my family").

Then, we can use this tense to focus on the result of a specific action, as in *Tú has lavado la ropa*. Here, the clean clothes result from washing them, so a past action has repercussions in the present.

Finally, this verb appears in sentences that give evidence of a past action, as in the example phrase *Este viaje ha sido increíble* ("This trip has been incredible") or in *Este masaje ha sido muy relajante* ("This massage has been very relaxing").

Revision of The Conditional Tense

After we visited the museum, we strolled through the *Jardín de la Unión*, a plaza at the heart of the city, which is surrounded by lovely historical and cultural buildings.

"Do you remember what the conditional tense in Spanish was all about?" Paula asked me.

"Yeah, I think so," I replied. "Basically, the conditional tense is used to convey wishes, obligation, suggestions, or polite requests, and it's even used to hypothesize about future situations depending on the conditions that affect them. The endings we need to form this tense work on all three conjugations, and we only need to attach them at the end of the infinitive:

- *Yo amaría*
- *Tú amarías*
- *Usted/Él/Ella amaría*
- *Nosotros/as amaríamos*
- *Ustedes/Ellos/Ellas amarían"*

I also told Paula that there were three types of irregularities to consider:

- Some verbs of the second and third conjugation lose their ending vowels (E or I, respectively) and are replaced by the letter D → *tendría, pondría*
- Other verbs experience the same loss of vowels, but don't feature an extra D → *sabría, podría*
- Then, there are some verbs that lose the vowels AND the consonant that's located at the end of the root → *haría diría*

We then came up with example phrases for each type of expression:

- Wishes: **Me encantaría** *besarte* ("I would love to kiss you").
- Obligation: **Deberías** *estudiar otro idioma* ("You should study another language").
- Suggestions: **Podrías** *hablar con tu jefe sobre el tema* ("You could talk to your boss about it").

- Polite requests: *¿**Podrías** decirme la hora, por favor?* ("Could you tell me the time, please?")

Condicional compuesto

At the *Jardín de la Unión*, Paula had the most amazing idea: to buy tickets to a performance at the Teatro Juárez for that same night! After all, this lovely theater is located right in front of the plaza, so it was perfect timing. As we stood in line to get the tickets, my friend told me about another verb tense: the *condicional compuesto*.

"The *condicional compuesto,*" said Paula, "is used when we have a sentence that requires the *pretérito pluscuamperfecto* (because it's an action prior to another past event) and describes situations we are unsure or uncertain about. However, if we are sure of such an event, we have to use the *pluscuamperfecto.*"

Paula gave me these examples:

- CERTAINTY: *Cuando llegué a casa, vi que Mariana estaba cansada porque **había limpiado** muy intensamente* ("When I got home, I saw that Mariana was tired because she had cleaned very intensely.")
- UNCERTAINTY: *Cuando llegué a casa, vi que Mariana estaba cansada. ¿**Habría limpiado** muy intensamente?* ("When I got home, I saw that Mariana was tired. Would she have cleaned very intensely?")

"So," I said, "when we want to hypothesize about 'the past of the past,' the most grammatically correct thing to do is to use this compound conditional."

"Yup," replied Paula. "Remember that the *condicional simple* refers to a hypothetical present or the future of the past. For example, you can say *Cuando vi las nubes en el cielo supe que **llovería*** ('When I saw the clouds in the sky, I knew it would rain'). On the other hand, the *condicional compuesto* refers to the hypothetical past, as in *Si no hubiera llovido tanto no **habrían florecido** todas las plantas* ('If it had not rained so much, all the plants would not have bloomed'), but we'll see more examples of this in just a bit."

I noticed that *habría* looked like the *condicional simple* tense of *haber*, a remark Paula confirmed. So, the structure I needed to use this tense was the following:

[VERB *HABER* IN THE *CONDICIONAL SIMPLE* + PAST PARTICIPLE]

My friend helped me with all the conjugations of *haber*:

CONDICIONAL SIMPLE DE HABER	
Yo	*habría*
Tú	*habrías*
Él/Ella/Usted	*habría*
Nosotros/Nosotras	*habríamos*
Ustedes	*habrían*
Ellos/Ellas	*habrían*

Revision of The Present Subjunctive

After getting the tickets to an orchestra, Paula suggested the next stop for the day:

"We should take a funicular ride to the Pipila Monument!" she said. "There are great panoramic views there."

However, it was already noon, so we stopped at a small family restaurant near the funicular. While we ate, Paula helped me review the present subjunctive tense because, apparently, it would be useful for learning more advanced topics.

When it came to the present subjunctive, I kind of remembered what it was about, so I tried to explain it to Paula to see if I was right.

"As far as I remember," I started saying, "the subjunctive is a way of expressing subjectivity, uncertainty, probability, desire, opinion, doubt, preferences, and emotions. We can also find this mood when we hear relative clauses, like the ones you taught me yesterday. That's why we often see the relative pronoun *que*, as in *Ojalá que llueva* ("I hope it rains"), and here's an example of how we can also use the subjunctive to talk about future events."

After my explanation, I looked on my phone for a chart with regular conjugations and another one with irregular examples:

SUBJUNTIVO PRESENTE	1°: amar → -e	2°: temer → -a	3°: partir → -a
que yo	ame	tema	parta
que tú	ames	temas	partas
que usted	ame	tema	parta
que él/ella	ame	tema	parta
que nosotros/nosotras	amemos	temamos	partamos
que ustedes	amen	teman	partan
que ellos/ellas	amen	teman	partan

IRREGULARES	Ser	Estar	Ver	Ir	Saber	Tener
que yo	sea	esté	vea	vaya	sepa	tenga
que tú	seas	estés	veas	vayas	sepas	tengas
que usted	sea	esté	vea	vaya	sepa	tenga
que él/ella	sea	esté	vea	vaya	sepa	tenga
que nosotros/nosotras	seamos	estemos	veamos	vayamos	sepamos	tengamos
que ustedes	sean	estén	vean	vayan	sepan	tengan
que ellos/ellas	sean	estén	vean	vayan	sepan	tengan

Then, Paula asked me to give her some example sentences, so I did:

- Wishes: *Espero que me **hagas** caso* ("I hope you will listen to me").
- Emotions: *Me preocupa que **te enfermes*** ("I'm worried you'll get sick").
- Impersonal sentences: *Es mejor que **nos quedemos** en casa* ("It is better to stay at home").
- Order/Request: *Te suplico que me **avises*** ("I beg you to let me know").
- Purpose: *Estudio para que me **contraten** mejores empresas* ("I study to be hired by better companies").
- Time: *Correré hasta que no **pueda** más* ("I will run until I can't run anymore").
- Doubt/Possibility: *Puede ser que **llueva** mañana* ("It may rain tomorrow").
- Opinions: *No creo que **tengas** piojos* ("I don't think you have lice").
- Taste/Preferences: *Odio que no me **escuches*** ("I hate that you don't listen to me").
- Relative sentences: *Mi madre necesita a alguien que la **cuide*** ("My mother needs someone to take care of her").

The Different Past Subjunctives

When the food came, Paula took the chance to teach me some past tenses the subjunctive mood has, which are really useful in everyday conversation.

Pretérito perfecto de subjuntivo

According to Paula, the *pretérito perfecto de subjuntivo* is used when the action from the subordinate clause (that is, the one that comes after the relative pronoun *que*) has been completed and its prior to the main sentence. The structure we need to use this tense is the following:

[VERB HABER (conjugated in the present subjunctive) + PAST PARTICIPLE (masculine singular form)]

Because I didn't know how to conjugate *haber* in the present subjunctive, Paula gave me a small chart, as always:

PRESENTE DE SUBJUNTIVO DE HABER	
Que yo	haya
Que tú	hayas
Qué él/ella/usted	haya
Que nosotros/nosotras	hayamos
Que ustedes	hayan
Que ellos/ellas	hayan

Here are a couple of sentences my friend told me:

- *Me encanta que **hayas cocinado** la cena* ("I love that you cooked dinner")
- *No creo que la función **haya empezado** todavía* ("I don't think the show has started yet")
- *¡Espero que te **haya gustado** el regalo!* ("I hope you liked the gift!")

The verb of the main sentence can be conjugated in the present, the *pretérito perfecto compuesto*, the future, or in the imperative. However, apparently, there are changes in meaning depending on the verb we use. For example, when the main sentence is in the present or past perfect tense, then the verb in the past perfect subjunctive expresses a past action. However, when the main sentence is in the future or imperative, then the subordinate clause expresses a future event:

- *Avísame cuando **hayas llegado** a casa* ("Let me know when you have arrived home")
- *Podrán hacer preguntas cuando la presentación **haya finalizado*** ("Questions may be asked after the presentation has ended")

Pretérito imperfecto de subjuntivo

When we finished eating, we asked for the check and went to the funicular (a cable railway on the mountainside) to buy some tickets. As we waited to board the vehicle, Paula taught me about the *pretérito imperfecto de subjuntivo*. According to Paula, we use this past subjunctive to express **imaginary or improbable events**, as well as wishes, emotions, doubts, or advice. The *pretérito imperfecto de subjuntivo* is equivalent to both the *pretérito perfecto simple* (*yo fui*) and the *pretérito imperfecto del indicativo* (*yo era*).

The *pretérito imperfecto* is used in almost the same cases in which we use the present subjunctive, only the sentence is in the past tense. For example:

- *Te pido que me ayudes* ("I ask you to help me")
- *Te pedí que me **ayudaras*** ("I asked you to help me")
- Espero que no haga frío ("I hope it won't be cold")
- Esperaba que no **hiciera** frío ("I hoped it wouldn't be cold")
- Me gusta que vayamos de picnic ("I like that we are going on a picnic")
- Me gustó que **fuésemos** de picnic ("I liked that we were going on a picnic")

Paula told me that this subjunctive tense was a bit more difficult than the perfect subjunctive because of its many irregularities. However, there are two endings that can be used indistinctively: **-ARA** or **-ASE** (for the first conjugation) or **-IERA** or **-IESE** (for the second and third conjugations). These need to be added to the root of the verb we want to use, as in *amara/amase*. Of course, we have different verb endings depending on the subject we want to use:

- *Que yo amara/amase*
- *Que tú amaras/amases*
- *Qué él/ella amara/amase*
- *Que nosotros/as amáramos/amásemos*
- *Que ustedes amaran/amasen*

To form the *pretérito imperfecto de subjuntivo* with the **-ARA** or -**IERA** endings, we can follow a simple rule that always works: we take the third person plural (*ellos*) of the *pretérito perfecto simple* (regular or irregular) of the verb we want to conjugate and change the vowel of the last syllable (*-ron* for *-ran*):

PRETÉRITO PERFECTO SIMPLE DEL MODO INDICATIVO	PRETÉRITO IMPERFECTO DEL MODO SUBJUNTIVO
Ellos/as fueron	Que ellos/as fueran
Ellos/as tuvieron	Que ellos/as tuvieran
Ellos/as pidieron	Que ellos/as pidieran

I was a bit worried about the irregular verbs to be honest, but Paula assured me that irregular verbs in the *pretérito perfecto simple* are also irregular in the *pretérito imperfecto de subjuntivo*. She gave me many examples in the third person plural:

INFINITIVO	PRET. PERF. SIMPLE (IND)	PRET. IMPERFECTO (SUBJ)
Ir	Ellos/as fueron	Que ellos/as fueran/fuesen
Ser	Ellos/as fueron	Que ellos/as hicieran/hiciesen
Estar	Ellos/as estuvieron	Que ellos/as estuvieran/estuviesen
Tener	Ellos/as tuvieron	Que ellos/as tuvieran/tuviesen
Hacer	Ellos/as hicieron	Que ellos/as hicieran/hiciesen
Poner	Ellos/as pusieron	Que ellos/as pusieran/pusiesen

Pretérito pluscuamperfecto de subjuntivo

On our way to the top, I could see every building in Guanajuato getting smaller and smaller every second, and the people looked like ants in a maze. It was a real spectacle, which got even better when we could see the city from a panoramic view.

When we were up there, Paula kept on with her explanation about the past subjunctive. She told me that this type of subjunctive is used to describe an impossible situation, which we cannot change anymore because the moment to do so has already passed. The necessary structure is:

[VERB *HABER* (conjugated in the *pretérito imperfecto de subjuntivo*) + PAST PARTICIPLE]

PRETÉRITO IMPERFECTO DE SUBJ. DE HABER	
Que yo	*hubiera/hubiese*
Que tú	*hubieras/hubieses*
Qué él/ella/usted	*hubiera/hubiese*
Que nosotros/nosotras	*hubiéramos/hubiésemos*
Que ustedes	*hubieran/hubiesen*
Que ellos/ellas	*hubieran/hubiesen*

In short, if we want to express a present desire, we need the *subjuntivo presente*: *Quiero que llueva* ("I want it to rain"). Then, if it is a desire expressed in the past, we will use:

- the **pretérito perfecto** if the past moment has not been concluded
  - *Ojalá mi hijo haya hecho su tarea* ("I hope my son has done his homework")

• the *pretérito imperfecto* if the past moment has been concluded

  ○ *Yo esperaba que ellos hicieran su trabajo* ("I was expecting them to do their job")

• and the *pluscuamperfecto* if we speak of a past action prior to another past event

  ○ *¡No te hubieras molestado!* ("You wouldn't have bothered!")

After a lovely afternoon, we went back to the hotel to get changed for the big event: the orchestra at the Teatro Juárez! Luckily, I had brought a summer suit just for this special occasion!

The Subjunctive and The Conditional Working Together

After getting dressed, my friend Paula (who looked stunning, by the way) started explaining the last grammar topic for that Tuesday: conditional sentences. Paula taught me how to come up with different conditional sentences, similar to the ones we already have in English, where each one has its own specific structure. This is what she told me on our way to the theater, on the line of the show, and on our seats, waiting for the show to start.

Condicionales tipo 1

Type-1 conditional sentences express a condition of possible/actual realization and require the following verb structure:

[*SI* + PRESENT INDICATIVE + PRESENT/FUTURE INDICATIVE or IMPERATIVE]

You can also replace the word *si* ("if." not "yes") with *cuando*. Paula gave me some key examples for me to consider:

• *Cuando yo **hablo** contigo, **aprendo** español* ("When I talk to you, I learn Spanish")

• *Si **tomas** mucho café, no **podrás** dormir* ("If you drink too much coffee, you won't be able to sleep")

• *Si **te sientes** mal, ¡**pide** el día libre en el trabajo!* ("If you feel bad, ask for a day off at work!")

Condicionales tipo 2

Type-two conditional sentences express a condition of unlikely/impossible realization and feature the following structure:

[*SI + PRETÉRITO IMPERFECTO DE SUBJUNTIVO + CONDICIONAL SIMPLE*]

Here are some examples:

- *Si **ganara** más dinero, **me compraría** una casa* ("If I earned more money, I would buy myself a house")
- *Si no **me parecieras** simpático, no **hablaría** contigo* ("If I didn't think you were nice, I wouldn't talk to you")
- *Si ser vegano no **fuera** tan caro, definitivamente lo **sería*** ("If being vegan were not so expensive, I would definitely be one")

Apparently, there's a variant of this type of conditional, where we show what would have happened in the past if something that is not true now and was not true before were different. For this, we need a slightly different verb structure:

[*SI + PRETÉRITO IMPERFECTO DE SUBJUNTIVO + CONDICIONAL COMPUESTO*]

Here are a couple of examples:

- *Si yo **fuera** vegetariana, no me **habría comido** todos esos tacos al pastor, ¿no?* ("If I were a vegetarian, I wouldn't have eaten all those tacos al pastor, would I?")
- *Si no **fuera** tan tímido, le **habría dicho** a Ana de salir conmigo* ("If I wasn't so shy, I would have told Ana to go out with me")
- *Si no **ganara** tan mal, te **habría comprado** un regalo más bonito* ("If I didn't have such a lousy salary, I would have bought you a nicer present")

Condicionales tipo 3

When we got to our seats, Paula explained the last conditional. Type-three conditional sentences express a condition of impossible realization (because they speak of the past, of things we can no longer change). To make them, we need to use the following structure:

[*SI + PRETÉRITO PLUSCUAMPERFECTO DE SUBJUNTIVO + CONDICIONAL COMPUESTO*]

For example, one could say *Si no hubiese conocido a tu madre, tú no habrías nacido* ("If I hadn't met your mother, you wouldn't have been born"). We can also use this type of conditional to talk about regrets we have in life, as in the sentence *Si **hubiera sabido** que ayer fue tu cumpleaños, te **habría dicho** algo* ("If I had known that yesterday it was your birthday, I would have said something")

Another alternative to this type of conditionals involves sentences that show how our lives would be like now if something different had occurred in our past, like this:

[*SI + PRETÉRITO PLUSCUAMPERFECTO DE SUBJUNTIVO + CONDICIONAL SIMPLE*]

These are the sentences Paula told me to help me understand:

- *Si **hubiese nacido** en México, hoy **sería** mexicano* ("If I had been born in Mexico, today I would be Mexican")
- *Si **hubiese estudiado** ingeniería, hoy no te **enseñaría** español, sino matemáticas* ("If I had studied engineering, today I would not teach you Spanish, but math")

"*¡Shhh!*" said Paula with her index finger over her mouth. "The show is about to begin!"

Mexican Cultural Annex

The evening was truly wonderful and magical as well. The musicians were so talented! I was blessed to have witnessed something like this. Given I was so moved by what I had just heard, Paula recommended two talented musicians who were from Guanajuato:

- **José Alfredo Jiménez (1926-1973):** he was a singer and prolific composer. He was considered one of the greatest musicians of *ranchera* music, a live performance that earned him the title of *El Rey de la Canción Ranchera* ("The king of the *ranchera* song"). One of his most popular songs is called "Camino de Guanajuato."
- **Jorge Negrete (1911-1953):** he was a singer, *ranchera* musician, and actor – and was known for his roles in the golden age of Mexican cinema. People remembered him for his charisma and talent. One of his most famous songs is "La Feria de las Flores."

Chapter Summary

Before turning off the lights in my hotel room, I did a little recap of what I had learned:

- First, I focused on two past tenses of the indicative mood: the *imperfecto progresivo* and the *pretérito perfecto compuesto*.

- Second, I revised how the *condicional simple* worked and saw another tense called *condicional compuesto*.

- Then, Paula helped me remember what the present subjunctive consisted of and taught me three past tenses of the subjunctive mood: the *pretérito perfecto,* the *pretérito imperfecto* and the *pretérito pluscuamperfecto*.

- Finally, I learned how to make three types of conditional sentences to reflect upon my past and my regrets.

Exercises

1. Complete the following sentences using the *imperfecto progresivo*.

    a. *Yo _____ (caminar) por la calle cuando escuché un ruido.*

    b. *Marcelo _____ (volver) a casa cuando se encontró con Tomás.*

    c. *¡Te _____ (decir) que te amaba cuando te quedaste dormido!*

    d. *Ellos _____ (vivir) en Japón cuando sucedió lo del tsunami.*

2. Complete the following sentences using the *pretérito perfecto compuesto*.

    a. *¿_____ (probar - tú) la comida polaca? Es muy buena.*

    b. *Yo nunca _____ (viajar) a las Islas Caimanes.*

    c. *Ellos _____ (trabajar) en este restaurante desde hace 5 años.*

    d. *Los turistas extranjeros nunca _____ (ver) un animal tan extraño.*

3. Decide whether the following sentences are right or wrong. Correct the wrong ones.

    a. *Si yo soy rico, viajaría por el mundo.*

    b. *¿Qué harías si tuvieras solo un día más de vida?*

c. *Si Juan habría estudiado para sus exámenes, hubiese aprobado.*

d. *Me encantarías conocer Florencia.*

4. Decide whether the following statement is true or false. If it's false, correct it.

Type-three conditionals are used for possible scenarios.

5. Translate the following conditional sentences:

a. "If I had more money, I would buy a house on the beach."

b. "What would you have studied if you hadn't been a doctor?

c. "When Ana Clara studies hard, she passes all her tests."

d. "If you are feeling sad, watch your favorite TV show!"

3. *Miércoles: Lo que nos depara el futuro*

"*¡Arriba, arriba!*" said Paula from outside my door as she knocked with insistence. "We've got a big day ahead of us!"

I knew Paula was right: that morning, we had to leave for Querétaro, a city also known for its well-kept colonial and baroque architecture. This place features many temples and churches, as well as museums and a surprising pink stone aqueduct. Given it was a three-hour drive, we were able to learn a lot of Spanish topics along the way!

Revision of *Futuro Simple* and *Futuro Perifrástico*

Since I already knew everything about el *futuro simple* and el *future perifrástico* from my previous trips, Paula asked me to explain these two tenses to her. This is what I remembered.

Futuro Simple

We drove into the highway with excitement and with our bellies full of breakfast! In that state of bliss, Paula started her explanation about the *futuro simple*:

"We use *futuro simple*," said Paula, "to talk about plans for the future and predictions and to speculate. It's equivalent to the use of 'will' in English. It's really easy to conjugate regular verbs in this tense: just add an ending to the infinitive of the verb. These endings depend on the person performing the action, of course, but they are the same for all conjugation: verbs ending in *-ar, -er,* and *-ir* take the same ending!"

Apparently, we add *-é* for the first person singular; we add *-ás* for the second person informal; we add *-á* for the second person formal and the third person singular; we add *-emos* for the first person plural; and we add *-án* for the second and third person plural. I used the verb *aprender* ("to learn") as an example:

- *Yo aprenderé*
- *Tú aprenderás*
- *Usted aprenderá*
- *Él aprenderá*
- *Ella aprenderá*
- *Nosotros aprenderemos*
- *Nosotras aprenderemos*
- *Ustedes aprenderán*
- *Ellos aprenderán*
- *Ellas aprenderán*

The future tense is one of the simplest tenses to learn in Spanish, and for that reason, I really liked it. However, as always, there are exceptions. In this case, the endings always stay the same, and the irregularities take place in the root. There are three types of irregularities in the future simple.

The verbs *decir* ("to say") and *hacer* ("to do") completely change their root before adding the future ending. *Decir-* becomes *dir-* and *hacer-* becomes *har-*. And we add the ending to these new roots:

- *Ellas **dirán** todo lo que saben* ("They will say everything they know").
- ***Haremos** la tarea* ("We'll do our homework").

Then, there are some verbs that change the vowel of their infinitive ending for a D. For example, *tener-* becomes *tendr-*. Then, the future ending is added to this new root:

- *Paula **pondrá** su casa a la venta* ("Paula will put her house for sale").
- *El viernes **saldremos** temprano para San Miguel de Allende* ("Early on Friday we'll leave for San Miguel de Allende").

- **_Tendremos_** _cuidado en el camino_ ("We'll be careful on the road").

- ¿**_Valdrá_** _la pena visitar la Parroquia de San Miguel Arcángel?_ ("Will it be worth visiting the Parroquia de San Miguel Arcángel?").

- _En seguida_ **vendrá** _el camarero a tomar su pedido_ ("The waiter will take your order right away").

Finally, there's a small group of verbs that drop the vowel of the infinitive ending before adding the future ending. For example, _poder-_ becomes _podr-_:

- _Allí no_ **cabrá** _mi maleta_ ("My bag won't fit there").

- ¿**Habrá** _dormido bien Paula?_ ("I wonder if Paula slept well").

- _Hoy fue un día largo, pero esta noche_ **podré** _descansar_ ("Today was a long day, but tonight I will be able to rest").

- ¿**Sabrán** _español esos turistas de ahí?_ ("I wonder if those tourists know Spanish?").

Paula was very happy with my explanation of the _futuro simple_. Before letting me move on to the _futuro perifrástico_, she wanted to add something:

"Remember that, in this tense, the reflexive pronoun of reflexive verbs, that is, _me, te, se, nos_ and _se_, goes before the verb. For example: _No_ **te** _olvidarás de este viaje._"

Futuro Perifrástico

While we were still on the road, I went on to explain the _futuro perifrástico_, the tense we use to talk about the near future, to express evident future facts, and to express a logical result. It's the equivalent of the English "going to." And, in fact, it's even easier than the simple future. Apparently, in Spanish, talking about the future is way simpler than talking about the past!

This is the structure to form the _futuro perifrástico_:

the verb _ir_ ("to go") in the present simple + the preposition _a_ + the verb that carries the meaning in the infinitive

In this construction, _ir_ works as an auxiliary verb, and the tense and person conjugations fall on it. The second verb, the one that stays in the infinitive, is the one carrying the meaning of the action. These are the examples I gave Paula:

- *Mañana **vamos a ir** al Museo Regional de Querétaro* ("Tomorrow, we are going to go to the Querétaro Regional Museum").

- *El sábado **voy a visitar** la Casa Museo Allende, en San Miguel de Allende* ("On Saturday, I'm going to visit the Casa Museo Allende, in San Miguel de Allende").

- *Si nos levantamos temprano, **vamos a tener** tiempo de hacer todo* ("If we wake up early, we are going to have time to do everything").

Present Simple to Talk About the Future

Half of the trip had passed, so it was time I explained one of the uses of the present simple: talking about the future. That's right, just as in English we say, "The train leaves tomorrow at 10," in Spanish we can say *El tren parte mañana a las 10*, using a verb in the present tense. This tense is used to talk about future events and actions that are certain. To indicate that they are going to happen in the future, we need to add a time marker. Here are some examples:

- *El lunes **llego** a Los Ángeles* ("On Monday, I arrive in Los Angeles").

- *¿A qué hora **despega** el avión?* ("What time does the plane take off?").

Future Times Markers

To finish my revision of the future tenses (because we were about to arrive in Querétaro), Paula asked me to tell her some future time markers, and these were the ones I could think of:

- *mañana* ("tomorrow")

- *mañana por la mañana, tarde, noche* ("tomorrow morning, afternoon, evening")

- *pasado mañana* ("the day after tomorrow")

- *la semana, el mes, el año que viene* ("next week, month, year")

- *dentro de un mes, un año* ("within a month, year")

- *pronto* ("soon")

- *dentro de poco* ("in no time")

- *más tarde* ("later")

- *ahorita* (this a very common word in Mexican Spanish. It means "now" or "right now").

"We have arrived in Santiago de Querétaro!" Paula said.

Futuro Compuesto

As we entered the city, its beauty became more and more evident. The traditional colonial buildings allowed us to enjoy the clear-blue sky that welcomed us on that lovely day. After checking into our new hotel, we set out to explore the historic center. Our first stop that day was the Plaza de Armas, a colonial square with a lovely fountain where the water splashes from dog sculptures!

While we were there, Paula said:

"Well, my friend, now that I'm sure that you understand the basic future tenses, it's time to introduce you to a new one: *futuro compuesto*." And so Paula began her explanation.

The perfect future or *futuro compuesto* belongs to the indicative mood, and it has two main uses.

It's used to talk about a future action that will end before another future action:

- *Para esa hora, ya **habremos llegado** a San Miguel de Allende* ("By that time, we will have already arrived in San Miguel de Allende").

And it's used to make assumptions of what might have happened in the past:

- *El chofer no ha llegado. **Se habrá demorado** en el camino* ("The driver hasn't arrived. He was probably delayed on the road").

Since it's a compound tense, it's made up of two verbs, an auxiliary and a main verb:

the verb *haber* in the simple future + the participle of the main verb

Lucky for me, I already knew everything about the participle! Paula added that, just as it happens with the simple future, the reflexive pronoun of reflexive verbs goes before the verb, as we had seen in one of the examples: *Se habrá demorado en el camino.*

After the explanation, we thought of some examples together. First, we thought of things that would happen or exist in the future, but before another thing happened:

- *Cuando vuelva a Estado Unidos, George **habrá aprendido** a hablar español como un nativo* ("When he returns to the United States, George will have learned to speak Spanish like a native").

- *A fin de año, Paula **habrá cambiado** de trabajo* ("At the end of the year, Paula will have changed jobs").

- *Para el año 2030, la población mundial **habrá alcanzado** los 8.600 millones de personas* ("By 2030, the world population will have reached 8,6 billion people").

- *Cuando llegue a la fiesta, tú ya **te habrás ido*** ("When I get to the party, you'll have left").

Then, we thought of examples of assumptions in the past:

- *Paula parece cansada, **habrá pasado** una mala noche* ("Paula looks tired, she must have had a bad night's sleep").

- *No encontramos nuestra tarjeta de embarque, la **habremos perdido*** ("We can't find our boarding pass, we've probably lost it").

- *George está bronceado, **se habrá ido** de vacaciones a la playa* ("George is tan, he probably went on vacation to the beach").

- *Me duele el estómago, **habré comido** algo que me hizo mal* ("I have a stomachache, I must have eaten something that made me sick").

Verbs that Take Direct Object

After walking around the Plaza de Armas, we went to a monument called Monumento a la Corregidora, which honored Josefa Ortiz de Domínguez. Paula said she had a key role during Mexico's independence, but she would tell me about it later when she remembered the story. There was a metal sculpture of a strong woman holding a torch, which looked really inspiring. While we kept on taking a stroll, Paula continued with her explanation.

The *objeto directo* or *complemento directo* of a sentence is the person or thing that receives the action of the verb, that is, the person or thing directly affected by the verb.

In Spanish, transitive verbs require a direct object to complete their meaning. Without the direct object, the meaning of the verb is not full. Paula gave me these examples to illustrate this idea:

- *El rey murió* ("The king died").
- *El rey mató* ("The king killed").

The difference is clear: in the first sentence, the meaning of the verb (an intransitive verb) is complete and in the second one, we are missing who or what the king killed, i.e., the direct object.

The Direct Object

The direct object is always a noun or a noun phrase, for example:

- *Juan bebe **agua*** (a noun).
- *Juan bebe **el tequila que le gusta*** (a noun phrase).

If the direct object refers to a person, a pet, or an animated being, it begins with the preposition *a*:

- *Contrataremos **a Silvia** para el puesto* ("We'll hire Silvia for the position").
- *El asesino mató **a las niñas*** ("The murderer killed the girls").

If the direct object refers to any other thing, it has no preposition:

- *¡Perdí **el vuelo**!* ("I lost my flight!").
- *George compró **muchos regalos*** ("George bought many presents").

The direct object can be replaced by objective pronouns *la, lo, las* or *los*:

- ***La** contrataremos para el puesto.*
- *El asesino **las** mató.*
- *¡**Lo** perdí!*
- *George **los** compró.*

Paula pointed out that, as it was clear from the examples, the pronoun comes before the verb.

Sometimes, the direct object can be duplicated:

- ***La** contrataremos **a Silvia** para el puesto.*

Transitive Verbs

I was still a bit confused about transitive verbs, the ones that require a direct object. Luckily, Paula gave me some tips for recognizing them:

"It's really easy, George. All you need to do is ask the verb the questions *¿qué?* ("what") or *¿a quién?* ("who") to determine if it has a direct object. Take a look at these examples."

- *Paula tiene dos gatos. ¿Qué tiene Paula? Dos gatos (The direct object is dos gatos).*
- *Mientras leo, cuido a mis hijos. ¿A quién cuido? A mis hijos (The direct object es a mis hijos).*

Then, Paula gave me a list of the most common transitive verbs:

- *adquirir* ("to acquire").
- *comer* ("to eat").
- *conocer* ("to know").
- *deber* ("to owe").
- *decir* ("to say").
- *encender* ("to turn on").
- *encontrar* ("to find").
- *matar* ("to kill").
- *poner* ("to put").
- *preparar* ("to prepare").
- *proponer* ("to propose").
- *querer* ("to want").
- *quitar* ("to remove").
- *romper* ("to break").
- *saber* ("to know").
- *tener* ("to have").
- *tomar* ("to take").
- *ver* ("to see").

Verbs that take indirect object

After grabbing a quick bite for lunch, we decided to go to the aqueduct on foot. It was a bit far away, but it gave us a chance to get to know the city and learn some more Spanish topics along the way.

According to Paula, the *objecto indirecto or complemento indirecto* of a sentence is the person or thing that receives the direct object through the direct object. The indirect object can appear with both transitive and intransitive verbs.

- *Todos los años, Paula dona cosas que ya no usa **a un hogar de niños*** ("Every year, Paula donates things she no longer uses to a children's home").

• *A George le gusta México* ("George likes México").

In the first sentence, we have a transitive verb (*donar*) with a direct object (*cosas que ya no usa*) and an indirect object (*a un hogar de niños*). In the second one, we have an intransitive verb (*gustar*) with an indirect object (*A George*), which is duplicated with the indirect object pronoun *le*.

The Indirect Object

We finally got to the aqueduct. It was incredible and surprisingly big! While we explored the area and took pictures, Paula continued with her explanation.

Apparently, the indirect object is introduced by the preposition *a*:

• *George compró regalos **a sus amigos*** ("George bought gifts for his friends").

• *Paula enseña español **a George*** ("Paula teaches George Spanish").

The indirect object can be replaced by indirect object pronouns *le* or *les*:

• *Todos los años, Paula **les** dona cosas que ya no usa.*

• ***Le** gusta México.*

• *George **les** compró regalos.*

• *Paula **le** enseña español.*

Again, the pronoun comes before the verb. And, when the direct object is also replaced by a pronoun, *le* and *les* become *se*:

• *Todos los años, Paula **se las** dona.*

• *George **se los** compró.*

• *Paula **se** lo enseña.*

It's common for the indirect object to be duplicated:

• *George **les** compró regalos **a sus amigos.***

• *Paula **le** enseña español **a George.***

Transitive Verbs that can Take an Indirect Object

After our visit, we decided to head back to our hotel, but Paula wanted to teach me something before we arrived:

"These are some of the transitive verbs that often have a direct and an indirect object," she said before making this list of words:

- *comunicar* ("to communicate").
- *contar* ("to tell").
- *dar* ("to give").
- *deber* ("to owe").
- *denunciar* ("to report").
- *entregar* ("to deliver").
- *hacer* ("to do").
- *llevar* ("to take").
- *ofrecer* ("to offer").
- *pagar* ("to pay").
- *poner* ("to put").
- *prender* ("to turn on").
- *prestar* ("to lend").
- *quitar* ("to take").
- *repartir* ("to distribute").
- *robar* ("to steal").
- *traer* ("to bring").

To all of these verbs, you can add the phrase *algo a alguien* ("something to somebody"), where *algo* is the direct object and *a alguien* the indirect object:

- *Les presté mi casa a unos amigos* ("I lent my house to some friends").
- *Le pagó la remera al cajero* ("He paid the cashier for the shirt").
- *A mis padres les robaron el auto* ("My parent's car was stolen").
- *Mi hermana me debe dinero* ("My sister owes me money").

Lo as a Neutral Pronoun

Before calling it a day, there was one more topic that Paula wanted to discuss with me: the neutral pronoun *lo*.

I already knew the function of pronouns: they replace nouns to avoid repetition. And, like many things in Spanish, they agree in gender and number with the noun they are replacing. However, Paula told me that there is a pronoun that isn't affected by gender: *lo*. This pronoun usually appears before an adjective or an adverb to function as a noun, as in:

- **Lo importante** *es estar sano y ser feliz* ("The important thing is to be healthy and happy")

- **Lo mejor** *de ser viejo es la jubilación* ("The best thing about being old is retirement")

- **Lo más interesante** *del libro es su narrador* ("The most interesting thing about this book is its narrator")

- *¡Me encanta* **lo** *dulce!* ("I love sweet things!")

Lo is used to talk about abstract notions or objects that aren't clearly defined. It can also be used to convey superlative ideas. Because this is a neutral pronoun, it cannot appear before a noun because this word always has an intrinsic gender that affects the other words around it. *Lo* can also refer to a previous sentence altogether, and it can be translated as "it" in English:

—*¿Ella necesita que la quieran?*
—*Sí,* **lo** *necesita.*

—*Debes estudiar más horas al día.*
—*Sí,* **lo** *sé.*

Relative Constructions with *lo*

Paula also taught me two relative constructions I could use with *lo*: *[lo + de +* noun*]* and *[lo + que +* verb*]*. The first structure can be used to talk about someone's house, and *lo* can be replaced by *la casa*. It can also be used to talk about a specific matter:

- *Mañana voy a* **lo de Laura** *después de la escuela* ("Tomorrow, I am going to Laura's after school")

- *Todos los fines de semana, vamos a* **lo de mi abuela** *a cenar* ("Every weekend, we go to my grandmother's for dinner")

- *¿Te enteraste de* **lo de Martín**? *Lo han despedido* ("Did you hear about Martin? He's been fired")

Then, the second relative structure with *lo* can be used to refer to a previously mentioned object or as a way of introducing a new clause:

- *Escucha* **lo que me dijo** *ayer mi madre* ("Listen to what my mother told me yesterday")

- *Esto no es* **lo que acordamos** ("This is not what we agreed")

Mexican Cultural Annex

At night, while we were having dinner, Paula remembered the story of "*La Corregidora*" Josefa Ortiz de Domínguez. She decided to tell me the story in Spanish so I could practice my listening skills:

María Josefa Ortiz de Domínguez fue una mujer clave en la lucha por la independencia del estado Mexicano contra la corona española. Ella nació en 1768 en Ciudad de México cuando el país se llamaba Nueva España. Sus padres pertenecían a una familia noble española, pero murieron cuando ella era solo una niña. De este modo, María Josefa fue criada por su hermana mayor, quien la ayudó a entrar a un prestigioso colegio. En ese entonces, conoció a su esposo, Miguel Domínguez, quien luego se convirtió en el corregidor de la ciudad de Querétaro. Los corregidores eran enviados del rey de España que supervisaban los virreinatos en las colonias.

Gracias a su clase y a su rol social, María Josefa fue conocida como "La Corregidora" y se involucró en las discusiones sobre la independencia de México. Casi es ejecutada por las autoridades realistas por complotar contra la corona, pero logró advertir a otros líderes independentistas, quienes apresuraron la lucha por la independencia.

Chapter Summary

Before hitting the sack, I wanted to do a brief recap of everything I had learned on that long day:

- First of all, we revised the *futuro simple* (*Yo* iré) and the *futuro perifrástico* (*Yo voy a ir*) tenses, we saw how we could use the present simple to talk about the future (*Mañana voy al médico*), plus some future time markers like *pronto* and *pasado mañana*. We then focused on the *futuro compuesto tense* and its uses.

- Second of all, Paula taught me how the direct object works and which transitive verbs can use this object in different scenarios.

- Then, Paula taught me the same thing but regarding indirect objects and transitive verbs for said objects.

- After that, we saw how *lo* works as a neutral pronoun.

- Finally, we focused on different constructions that included the neutral pronoun *lo*, as in the phrase *Lo que los humanos queremos es guerra.*

Exercises

1. Transform each sentence and make three future sentences, first with the *futuro simple,* then with the *futuro perifrástico,* and finally with the *futuro compuesto.*

   a. *Yo como tacos al pastor.*

   b. *¿Conseguiste un nuevo trabajo?*

   c. *A María Elena no le gustó la sorpresa.*

2. Come up with five sentences with a transitive verb and a direct object.

3. Come up with five sentences with an intransitive verb and an indirect object.

4. Decide whether the following sentences are right or wrong. Correct the wrong ones.

   a. *Lo malo de ir a su casa es que está muy lejos*

   b. *¿Qué son los buenos de tener un perro?*

   c. *Estas vacaciones fueron lo mejor que me pasó en la vida.*

   d. *Los peores de la fiesta fueron que hacía mucho calor y que la música era mala.*

5. Translate the following sentences by using a relative construction with *lo:*

   a. "What does she want this time?"

   b. "You forgot about what we once were."

   c. "Is this what you want to make of your life?"

4. Jueves: La gente anda diciendo...

Another day of adventures in Querétaro awaited us! That Thursday morning, after having a delicious breakfast at the hotel, we went to the Casa de la Corregidora, which is currently the seat of Querétaro's government. A tour guide took us inside the building and told us about its historical importance in Mexico's independence process.

At one point, the guide said:

"*Se* cree que Miguel Domínguez encerró a su esposa en un cuarto para protegerla."

I didn't want to interrupt the tour, so I wrote the phrase as best as I could and once the tour was over, I took out my notebook, read the phrase, and asked Paula, "What does *se* mean here?"

Paula told me that the phrase could be translated as "It is believed that Miguel Domínguez locked his wife in a room to protect her." And explained that, in this case, *se* was used to make the sentence impersonal.

Impersonal Constructions

Apparently, the example I brought up isn't the only way in which you can be impersonal in Spanish. But first, Paula explained that impersonal constructions are those phrases or sentences in which there is no concrete subject, and they are generally used to talk about people in general and not in particular.

Se + verb

The first way to be impersonal that Paula taught me is the one that led us to this topic: the use of *se*. Paula explained that there are several ways to use *se* in an impersonal construction.

Firstly, we can use *se* with a third-person singular verb to say something general, like:

- *En México se come rico* ("In Mexico people/you eat delicious food")

As you can see, in this kind of construction in English, we need to use a more specific subject, like "you" or "people," but in Spanish, we're not talking about anyone in particular; we are just stating a fact about Mexico, and so we use *se*.

Paula mentioned that this form is most generally used in proverbs or sayings, such as:

- *No se puede chiflar y comer pinole al mismo tiempo*

This literally means that you can't whistle and eat *pinole* at the same time. However, its figurative meaning is that sometimes one can't do everything but should learn to prioritize. Since this saying can be applicable to everyone and isn't personal, we use *se* + verb.

La gente / *uno* + verb indicative

Paula anticipated my possible questions and explained that whenever the verb already has *se* (as with reflexive verbs), we can't use impersonal *se* again, so we use *la gente* or *uno* as the subject to make it clear that we're not talking about anyone in particular.

When we use *la gente*, we, of course, mean people in general. For example:

- *En Francia, la gente se bañaba una vez al mes* ("In France, people used to bathe once a month")

When we use *uno* or *una*, we also mean people in general, but we can also use it when we want to state our own opinion in a seemingly neutral way. For example:

- *Una se divierte más con amigos* ("One has more fun with friends")
- *Uno se cansa rápido después de los 80* ("One gets tired quickly after 80")

Se + verb + *que* + indicative mood

When our tour of the Casa de la Corregidora was over, we went over to the Templo de Santa Rosa de Viterbo, with a tall tower and a huge dome to explore.

While I was thinking about Paula's explanation, I noticed that the sentence with *se* I had written down was a bit different because after the verb, there was a *que*, so I asked her how to use this other form, and she said that she was actually getting around to it.

So, Paula went on to explain that there is another formula to use impersonal *se*, which I wrote down like this:

se + verb + *que* + indicative mood

This form, she said, is especially used to talk about hearsay or rumors. Here are the examples that Paula gave me:

- *Se dice que los Rodríguez ganaron la lotería* ("It is said that the Rodriguez won the lottery")
- *Se sospecha que Carlos es el ladrón* ("It is suspected that Carlos is the thief")

In this form, we use *que* to introduce what it is said, suspected, believed, etc., and we use *se* because the person who says or suspects isn't someone in particular but people in general: it could be the whole family, neighborhood, state or even the whole world!

However, she explained that there are a few exceptions: when we use wish verbs, we have to change the indicative mood for the subjunctive. For example:

- *Se espera que mañana **llueva*** ("It is hoped that tomorrow will rain")

And this applies to all verbs that express a wish or hope.

hay + *que*

Then, Paula went on to explain that we also use the verb *haber* as impersonal. In this case, we use an invariable form of the third person singular, like *hay*, followed by *que* to make a general statement. For example:

- *Hay que ser agradecido* ("One has to be thankful")
- *Hay que cuidarse entre sí* ("We have to look out for each other")

Third Person Plural

Another interesting thing Paula mentioned is that sometimes sentences that feature a third-person plural subject can be interpreted as impersonal phrases, but their subject must be omitted, as these sentences show:

- *¡Llaman a la puerta!* ("There's a knock at the door!")
- *Dicen que esa casa está maldita* ("They say that house is haunted")

Active and Passive Voice

After our visit, it was time for us to enter the Museo Regional de Querétaro, an ex-colonial convent from the sixteenth century. As we were heading over there, I saw a small newsstand with many different newspapers. I don't know exactly why, but a special headline caught my attention:

100 puestos de trabajo fueron creados este jueves

"Paula, what does this mean?" I asked my friend with curiosity.

"It says, '100 job postings were created this Thursday'," replied Paula. "I believe we haven't talked about passive voice in Spanish yet, have we? This is a great chance to do it, then!"

Active Voice

Paula went up to the salesman and bought that newspaper I had seen. This is what I understood from Paula's explanation about active voice:

In most of the sentences we produce, we use the active voice because both Spanish and English usually follow the same structure: first, we name the subject, then the conjugated verb, and a direct object that is affected by said verb. However, for this object to appear, we need to use a transitive verb, which is an action that requires both a subject and an object to occur, as in:

- *Yo como tres tacos* (*Yo* = subject | *como* = verb | *tacos* = DO)
- *Ana* besa a Nicolás (*Ana* = subject | *besa* = verb | *Nicolás* = DO)

We talked about the direct object the day before, but the lesson was good for refreshing my memory.

On the contrary, intransitive verbs like *ser, estar,* and *sonreír* cannot be used in passive voice sentences because they don't admit a direct object. Going back to the examples, both *tres tacos* and *su esposo* are direct objects because they are the recipient of the action, or the action affects them directly. We call these objects **pacientes** ("patients") because of this. I also knew these were direct objects because they could be replaced by the pronouns *los* and *lo,* respectively:

- *Yo los como*
- *Ana lo besa*

When I asked Paula how she could tell these phrases were in the active voice, she told me that **the subject is the one who performs the action** described by the verb (I am the one eating tacos, and Ana is the one kissing Nicolás). When this happens, the subject is called the **agent.**

Passive Voice

"What about the passive voice, then?" I asked Paula when we had just entered the museum.

After nagging me about my impatience, she said that passive voice is like the other side of the coin. Passive voice is called that way because it displaces the agent from its privileged position within the sentence and **highlights the object (the *paciente*) instead.** This means that the subject of *passive* sentences is patients, not agents, as in the *active* ones. Because this new subject doesn't perform the action, we also need to change the verb we use:

- *Tres tacos <u>son comidos</u> por mí* ("Three tacos are eaten by me")
  - ○ *Tres tacos* = patient subject
  - ○ *son comidos* = passive verb
  - ○ *mí* = real agent)
- *Nicolás <u>es besado</u> por Ana* ("Nicolás is kissed by Ana")
  - ○ *Nicolás* = patient subject
  - ○ *es besado* = passive verb
  - ○ *Ana* = real agent)

I noticed that the pronoun *yo* no longer appeared in the passive voice sentence. Paula told me this worked like the verb *gustar*, where we say *A mí me gustan los tacos* instead of *A yo me gustan*. Then, the verbs' person and number have changed, too, because **they need to be in agreement** with the new subject.

"Now, the direct object is highlighted at the beginning of the sentence," I said to Paula. "But what about the previous subject? If it's not the subject anymore, what is it?"

My friend told me that these agents at the end of the sentences didn't become direct objects but now carry a different function, which is called *complemento agente* in Spanish. This complement specifies that the featured verb was performed by that agent and not the new passive subject. I could easily find this *complemento agente* within a passive phrase because it's introduced by the preposition *por* (we use "by" in English.)

In summary, this was the structure I had to learn to make passive sentences:

[PASSIVE SUBJECT + VERB *SER* CONJUGATED + ACTION VERB AS PARTICIPLE (former active verb) + *COMPLEMENTO AGENTE*]

This means verbs in the passive voice are compound verbs, including an auxiliary verb (conjugated in the necessary tense) and an action verb, as it happens in the *presente continuo* tense. Paula began to make examples in different tenses for me to incorporate the structure:

- *Presente simple: Tres tacos **son comidos** por mí* ("Three tacos are eaten by me")
- *Presente continuo: Tres tacos **están siendo comidos** por mí* ("Three tacos are being eaten by me")
- *Pretérito imperfecto: Tres tacos **eran comidos** por mí* ("Three tacos were eaten by me")
- *Imperfecto continuo: Tres tacos **estaban siendo comidos** por mí* ("Three tacos were being eaten by me")
- *Pretérito perfecto simple: Tres tacos **fueron comidos** por mí* ("Three tacos were eaten by me")
- *Pretérito pluscuamperfecto: Tres tacos **habían sido comidos** por mí* ("Three tacos had been eaten by me")
- *Futuro simple: Tres tacos **serán comidos** por mí* ("Three tacos will be eaten by me")
- *Futuro perifrástico: Tres tacos **van a ser comidos** por mí* ("Three tacos are going to be eaten by me")

- *Condicional simple: Tres tacos **serían comidos** por mí* ("Three tacos would be eaten by me")
- *Condicional compuesto: Tres tacos **habrían sido comidos** por mí* ("Three tacos would have been eaten by me")

I was a bit overwhelmed to be honest, but Paula told me that these were just examples, nothing more.

Then, I remembered that the participles we use next to the auxiliary verb *ser* need to agree in gender and number with this new passive subject:

- *Un taco es **comido** por mí*
- *Una banana es **comida** por mí*
- *Dos bananas son **comidas** por mí*

The only thing I have to do to create them is to remove the infinitive ending and add the suffix **-ADO** or **IDO** depending on which conjugation I want to use, plus the gender and number agreement. This only applies if the participle is regular, of course.

Now, one key thing one can do when using the passive voice is to omit the agent altogether. For example, If I said *Tres tacos fueron comidos*, no one would know it was me who did it, at least not because I confessed to it. Now, Paula told me to remember the headline I saw a couple of minutes earlier: *100 puestos de trabajo fueron creados este jueves* ("100 job postings were created this Thursday"). In this case, only by reading this sentence, we wouldn't be able to know who created these jobs. However, when I read the first paragraph of the article, I learned it was the local government, so the newspaper could have said *100 puestos de trabajo fueron creados por el gobierno este jueves.*

To my understanding, passive voice is common in places like journalism (and the media in general) because we can highlight a part of the sentence and hide what we don't want the audience to see. This is the example Paula gave to me for the second scenario:

"Imagine that the government did something bad, like closing a factory, and doesn't want to be explicitly named in the headline. In that case, a journal that supports the administration would say something like *La fábrica X fue cerrada* instead of just saying *El gobierno cerró la fábrica X*, because that would soften the blow a little more."

Paula's explanation made a lot of sense. She also told me that the passive voice is not that common in spoken Spanish, but that I could use it in formal contexts, such as letters of complaint or reports.

Direct and Indirect Speech

It was a lovely afternoon at the museum, but it was getting a bit dark outside, so we decided to head over to a park called Jardín Zenea, which had a huge metal gazebo and lovely fountains to enjoy.

Since we had that newspaper we had bought before entering the museum, Paula thought it would be nice to introduce another key grammar topic for advanced learners: direct and indirect speech. The first one was really straightforward:

"When using direct speech," Paula said, "we reproduce exactly what another person said, word for word, and we use quotation marks to highlight that that sentence wasn't ours. It is generally introduced by a verb of speech, such as *decir, afirmar, exclamar, declarar,* etc.. We usually find direct speech in interviews or direct profiles because the idea is to be respectful of what the special guest has said."

We then skimmed through the local newspaper until we found a couple of real-life examples of direct speech:

- *"Estamos trabajando para mejorar la vida de los ciudadanos",* **dijo** *el gobernador.*
- *El jefe de policía* **afirmó** *que "todavía no hay pruebas suficientes".*
- *"Aún no obtuvimos respuesta de las autoridades",* **declaró** *una de las vecinas afectadas.*

Paula then explained that sometimes we wish to reproduce what another person said but only through reformulation, that is, *paraphrasing the whole sentence altogether.* This can also be found in journalism and everyday conversation. For example, if you are telling an anecdote that involves other people and you want to say approximately what the conversation was about. In this case, because we aren't quoting, we won't need quotation marks, but we do need an introductory verb, so that people know we are not the ones saying it – but another person. Of course, if we want to use indirect speech, we are going to need to change a few things for our sentences to work properly. First of all, we need to change the pronouns and verbs used so that they are in agreement with the new subject. For example, if someone is talking in the first person, you will then need to address them in the third one:

- *"Yo no **como** carne", dice Andrea.* → *Andrea **dice** que **ella** no **come** carne.*

- *"**Nosotros** sabemos nadar muy bien", dicen los niños.* → *Los niños **dicen** que **ellos saben** nadar muy bien.*

The indirect speech part is introduced by the word *que*. According to Paula, we also need to be mindful of the possessives and demonstratives when switching from direct to indirect speech:

- *"¡Me encanta **mi** país!", dice Tobías.* → *Tobías dice que le encanta **su** país.*

- *"Yo siempre tomo café en **esta** taza", dice el señor.* → *El señor dice que siempre toma café en **esa** taza.*

This means that words like *aquí* have to be transformed into *allí*, and demonstratives like *este/a* will become *ese/a* or *aquel/aquella*. A similar thing happens with verbs that are determined by location, such as *ir/venir* and *llevar/traer*. Paula also told me that whenever I use indirect speech, I should pay attention to any time markers in the sentence because when it's removed from its original context, any references made would need to be changed for it to still make sense, like this:

- *"Ayer estaba en el médico", dice Kevin.* → *Kevin dice que **el día anterior** estaba en el médico.*

- *"La semana pasada había ido a verlo", dice Rita.* → *Rita dice que **la semana anterior** había ido a verlo.*

Here's a chart Paula gave me with all the changes in time expressions:

Estilo directo	*Estilo indirecto*
Hoy	*Aquel día*
Ayer	*El día anterior*
Anoche	*La noche anterior*
Ahora	*Entonces / En ese momento*
Mañana	*Al día siguiente*

La semana que viene	La semana siguiente
La semana pasada	La semana anterior

Finally, Paula told me that when the introductory verb is in *presente simple, futuro simple,* or *pretérito perfecto compuesto,* we don't need to change the tense of the other verbs, only the changes she had taught me:

- "Estoy bien", dice Tamara. → *Tamara dice que está bien.*

However, when we have an introductory verb in *pretérito perfecto simple, pretérito imperfecto,* or *pluscuamperfecto,* the verb tenses of the reported phrases must "go back one space" in the verb timeline, as in:

- "Estoy bien", dijo Tamara. → *Tamara **dijo** que **estaba** bien.*

"But how can I know which verb to use, then?" I asked Paula.

"*No te preocupes...*" replied Paula, and then handed me a chart with all the changes I needed to learn:

Estilo directo	Estilo indirecto	Ejemplo
Presente	Pretérito imperfecto	"Estoy enfermo", dijo Juan. → Juan dijo que **estaba** enfermo.
Pretérito indefinido	Pretérito pluscuamperfecto	"Estuve enfermo", dijo Juan.
Pretérito perfecto compuesto		→ Juan dijo que **había estado** enfermo.
Futuro simple	Condicional simple	"Estaré de viaje", dijo Ana. → Ana dijo que **estaría** de viaje.

Futuro compuesto	Condicional compuesto	"Habré perdido mis llaves", dijo Luis. → Luis dijo que **habría perdido** sus llaves.
Presente de subjuntivo	Pretérito imperfecto de subjuntivo	"No creo que llueva", me dijo Eva. → Eva me dijo que no creía que **lloviera.**
Pretérito perfecto de subjuntivo	Pretérito pluscuamperfecto de subjuntivo	"No hay nadie que me haya visto", dijo Hugo → Hugo dijo que no había nadie que lo **hubiera/hubiese** visto.

I was a bit overwhelmed, but luckily, Paula told me that some verb tenses do not experience changes when switching to passive voice:

Estilo directo	Estilo indirecto	Ejemplo
Pretérito imperfecto	Pretérito imperfecto	"Estaba enfermo", dijo Juan. → Juan dijo que **estaba** enfermo.
Pretérito pluscuamperfecto	Pretérito pluscuamperfecto	"Había llegado tarde", dijo Nina. → Nina dijo que **había llegado** tarde.
Condicional simple	Condicional simple	"Querría un refresco", dijo León. → León dijo que **querría** un refresco.

Condicional compuesto	*Condicional compuesto*	"Habría tenido frío", dijo Maia. → *Maia dijo que **habría tenido** frío.*
Pretérito imperfecto de subjuntivo	*Pretérito imperfecto de subjuntivo*	"Me **hubieras avisado** antes", dijo Xul. → *Xul dijo que le **hubiera avisado** antes.*

Then, Paula told me things got a bit more complex when it came to indirect questions – but that it wasn't so hard for me to learn. In the first place, she explained that whenever we see a question that features a question word like *cuándo, dónde, cómo,* etc., we should keep that word when switching to indirect speech:

- *"¿Cómo estás?", preguntó Claudia.* → *Claudia preguntó **cómo** estaba.*
- *"¿Cuándo vendrás a casa?", me preguntó mi mamá.* → *Mi mamá me preguntó **cuándo** iría a casa.*

However, if we are dealing with a yes or no question, the word *que* has to be replaced by *si*, without a *tilde*:

- *"¿Quieren pasar?", nos preguntó Flora.* → *Flora nos preguntó **si** queríamos pasar.*
- *"¿Tuvieron frío anoche?", nos preguntó Sergio.* → *Sergio nos preguntó **si** habíamos tenido frío la noche anterior.*

When dealing with sentences in the imperative mood, we should change them into the subjunctive:

- *"Come más", ordenó mi abuela.* → *Mi abuela ordenó que **comiera** más.*
- *"¡Vete de aquí!", gritó mi hermano.* → *Mi hermano gritó que **me fuera** de allí.*

Mexican Cultural Annex

Finally, Paula thought it would be nice to teach me a popular Spanish expression I could hear while walking down the streets of Mexico and

Latin America in general. This expression is **Dicen las malas lenguas** or **Las malas lenguas dicen**. This sentence is used to introduce rumors or negative comments surrounding a person or a place.

The literal translation would be "The evil tongues say," because the rumor comes from unreliable sources or from people who wish to cause trouble by spreading this information. In English, we usually say something like "Rumor has it":

- *Dicen las malas lenguas que Patri está embarazada* ("Rumor has it Paula is pregnant")

- *¡Las malas lenguas dicen que Tomás dejó a su mujer!* ("Rumor has it Tomás left his wife!")

Chapter Summary

After I went to bed, I decided to revise everything I've learned on that Thursday:

- First of all, we focused on the different ways of making impersonal constructions:
  - With the word *se* plus a verb, like in *Se venden cuadernos*.
  - With the formula *La gente/uno* + verb + *que* + indicative mood, like in *Uno nunca sabe lo que le depara el futuro*.
  - With the same formula but switching *la gente/uno* with *se*, like in *Se piensa que las mujeres son débiles, pero no lo son*.
  - With the verb *hay* plus the word *que*, like in *Hay que limpiar la casa*.
  - With the third person plural, like in *Dicen que ese restaurante está bueno*.
- Then, Paula taught me how to recognize and use the passive voice in different sentences, like in *El discurso es dicho por el presidente*.
- Finally, I learned about direct and indirect speech and how verbs get modified, like in *Me dijo que estaba triste*.

Exercises

1. Come up with one example sentence for each of the five ways of making impersonal phrases in Spanish.

2. Decide whether the following statement is true or false. If it's false, correct it.

    La gente, one of the ways of making impersonal sentences in Spanish, needs a verb in its plural form to be used.

3. Transform the following active phrases into the passive voice:

    a. *El hombre correrá a su perro en la avenida.*

    b. *Los sapos atrapan moscas cada mañana.*

    c. *¡Mis gatos destruyeron mi sillón de cuero!*

4. Decide whether the following statement is true or false. If it's false, correct it.

    The phrase *Yo trabajo como contador* can be transformed into the passive voice.

5. Transform the following sentences in direct speech into indirect speech:

    a. *"'¿Quieres comer con nosotros?', me preguntó Carla".*

    b. *"'¡Ayer vi a mi madre sola en el parque!', dijo Martín".*

    c. *"'Ven aquí', Carlos le ordenó a su hijo".*

    d. *"'Ojalá llueva', exclamó Susana".*

5. *Viernes: Tomárselo con calma*

Instead of a quiet vacation morning, I was awakened by a sudden lightning strike outside my hotel room. The noise the thunder made was so loud I remember almost falling out of my bed! It must have been about 6-ish in the morning, which was not so bad, but my restful sleep went down the drain.

I had no choice but to get out of bed because there was no way I could go back to sleep at that point.

"I wonder if Paula is awake too..." I thought.

Luckily, she was! The thunder got her out of bed, too, so we decided to take advantage of our rainy rise to grab an early breakfast and hit the road. That day, we had planned to travel to San Miguel de Allende, an old city known for its baroque architecture and cultural activities. It was only an hour away, and the highway was quite calm because of the time of day.

Revision of Reflexive Verbs

As we were driving, we took the opportunity to start with our Spanish lesson of the day. This time, we did a little review of reflexive verbs.

"You remember what reflexive verbs are, right?" Paula asked me.

"Yeah, I think I do," I replied. "Reflexive verbs are a type of pronominal verb that expresses an action that only affects the subject performing the action. For example, when I say *Yo me levanto*, I'm not doing anything to anyone but myself. We can recognize reflexive verbs in their bare form by their *-SE* ending, and when conjugated they become two separate words."

Then, I said the following sentences out loud:

- *Yo **me** siento bien.*
- *Tú **te** sientes bien.*
- *Usted **se** siente bien.*
- *Él **se** siente bien.*
- *Ella **se** siente bien.*
- *Nosotros **nos** sentimos bien.*
- *Nosotras **nos** sentimos bien.*
- *Ustedes **se** sienten bien.*
- *Ellos **se** sienten bien.*
- *Ellas **se** sienten bien.*

Reflexive Verbs with Modal Verbs

"Very good!" said Paula. "And what about when we want to use these verbs with another modal verb like *querer, necesitar, tener que,* or *poder?*"

"We have to use the reflexive verb in the infinitive, as only one word," I replied, "but the pronoun suffix needs to be in agreement in person and number with the subject, like in *Yo quiero levantar**me** temprano* or in *Necesitamos lavar**nos** las manos.*"

Reflexive Verbs in The Imperative Mood

"*¡Excelente!*" said Paula. "And what about when we want to give an order with the imperative mood?"

"It works in the same way as with the modal verbs," I said, "all you have to do is to change the verb into the imperative and then add the proper pronoun ending: *ponte cómodo* ('make yourself comfortable') or *siéntate derecho* ('sit up straight')."

Then, Paula helped me review which type of reflexive verbs there were:

1) Some reflexive verbs show the actions that the individual performs on himself:
   - *Acostarse*
   - *Levantarse*

- *Bañarse*
- *Ducharse*
- *Lavarse las manos/los dientes*
- *Cepillarse los dientes/el cabello*
- *Maquillarse*

2) Some reflexive verbs show a change of state or physical condition:
- *Acercarse (a)*
- *Alejarse (de)*
- *Despertarse*
- *Quedarse*
- *Dormirse*
- *Quedarse dormido/a*
- *Mudarse (de/a)*
- *Sentirse bien/mal*

3) Some reflexive verbs show a change of sensation or perception:
- *Acostumbrarse (a)*
- *Asegurarse (de)*

4) Some reflexive verbs show a change of status or social condition:
- *Enamorarse (de)*
- *Comprometerse (con)*
- *Casarse (con)*
- *Pelearse (con)*
- *Divorciarse (de)*

5) Some reflexive verbs show a change in emotional state:
- *Aburrirse*
- *Divertirse*
- *Deprimirse*
- *Alegrarse*

After a not-so-long drive, we arrived in San Miguel de Allende!

Passive voice with *se*

With picturesque low houses and cobblestone streets, San Miguel de Allende looked like a city from a different time, far removed from our fast-paced, technological present. However, rain was pouring down from every rooftop, and visibility was difficult.

"Thank goodness I packed my umbrella!" Paula said.

When we arrived at the hotel and checked in at the front desk, we quickly unpacked so we could head out to explore in the rain. Our destination was a parish called Parroquia de San Miguel Arcángel, known for its 17th-century neo-Gothic style, with tall pink towers and detailed ornaments.

Walking under our big red umbrella, Paula told me that she wanted to teach me more about the passive voice.

"I thought your explanation was excellent!" I told her.

"*¡Gracias!*" replied Paula, "but it wasn't as complete as I wanted it to be."

Paula began explaining what the passive voice with the pronoun *se* is. These types of sentences are also quite common in newspapers, especially in the classified section, because we use these sentences to further omit the subject of the featured verb, mostly because it is not really relevant or because the subject is multiple people with no connection between them other than doing the same thing. Paula gave me this example:

"Imagine you are an actor, and you're looking for potential roles. In that case, you might be interested in an ad that says: *Se buscan actores para comercial televisivo* ('Actors wanted for TV commercial'). Of course, someone is performing the action of *buscar* (like an advertising agency), but what's important is the search itself, not the people who are conducting it. This phrasing is a good resource for a small advertising agency whose name is not relevant, so they want to highlight the job advert instead of themselves. The verbs that appear are in the third person, singular or plural, and they have to be transitive verbs because we are talking about a passive sentence."

In short, the passive voice with *se* can be formed with the following structure:

After Paula's explanation, I wanted to find an example sentence myself. After we arrived at the foot of the parish, we found shelter under a small stone roof, so I took out my cell phone, went online, and started looking at the classified section of the local newspaper. After a while, I found this:

Se vende casa de veraneo

*Se oferta una bonita casa cerca de la
playa.
Dos habitaciones, un baño, cocina y sala
de estar.
¡Perfecta para disfrutar de las vacaciones en
familia!*

When I translated this with Paula, we ended up with "Holiday home for sale. Nice house near the beach is offered. Two bedrooms, one bathroom, kitchen, and living room. Perfect for family holidays!"

Passive voice with *estar*

The interior hall of the parish was simply breathtaking, with vaulted ceilings and crystal chandeliers. While we were there, Paula lowered her voice and told me that there is a third type of passive sentence, one that requires the use of the verb *estar*. This is apparently really useful when we want to describe the state of something. For example, Paula provided some examples related to a date with her husband at their place:

- *La casa **está ordenada*** ("The house is tidied up")
- *Las luces **están apagadas*** ("The lights are turned off")
- *Las velas **están encendidas*** ("The candles are lit")
- *La cena **está servida*** ("Dinner is served")
- *La cama **está tendida*** ("The bed is made")

"But someone decided for these things to be this way," I said. "Candles don't just happen to be lit on their own..."

"You are right," Paula said, "in these cases, someone made everything flawless, but there are other passive sentences with *estar* where this doesn't apply, like in *El reloj está roto* ('The watch is broken'). Maybe someone broke the watch, but it could have also broken on its own, right?"

"That's true..." I replied. "But *can* we mention the subject of the action with this structure?"

"Well, we can..." said Paula, "but only when that agent, whether it is a person, an animal, or a weather phenomenon, is still affecting the object in question, like in *La salida está bloqueada por guardias* ('The exit is blocked by guards')."

Paula also told me that there are some exceptions to this structure of *estar* + participle. For instance, sometimes we use an adjective instead of a participle, like in *Los vasos están **limpios*** instead of *limpiados*.

After we left the parish, it was raining cats and dogs, so we had to gather all the courage we could find and venture into the flooded streets ("streets" was a generous name: the main road looked like a stream on which boats could sail). With soggy shoes, we went back to our hotel, for it wasn't a day to roam around the city. Despite that unfortunate turn of events, our afternoon wasn't that bad at all: the hotel had a lovely bistro, so we sat down to have a drink and continue with the Spanish lessons.

Morphology and Uses of Relative Adverbs and Pronouns

We ordered two gin and tonics, and the lesson began.

Relative Adverbs

"Do you know what relative adverbs are, George?" Paula asked me.

"I think so," I replied. "I believe that relative adverbs are words that appear at the beginning of a relative clause, which are subordinate clauses we use to add extra information about a person, place, object, etc.. Relative adverbs can express location *(donde / adonde)*, quantity *(cuanto/cuan)*, time *(cuando)* and manner *(como)*. They help us introduce a new sentence with <u>a conjugated verb</u>, like in *Yo voy **adonde** tenga ganas* ('I go wherever I feel like it')."

"*¡Excelente!*" said Paula.

She then proceeded to give me a couple more examples:

- *Yo aprendí a leer **cuando** <u>tenía</u> cinco años* ("I learned to read when I was five")
- *Yo comí **cuanto** <u>quise</u>* ("I ate as much as I wanted")

- *Ellos bailan **como** les enseñó su maestro* ("They dance like their teacher taught them")

Relative Pronouns

When Paula told me we were going to talk about relative pronouns, I asked her if she would let me try to explain them before she did. I studied these types of pronouns back home and wanted to check whether I understood them or not:

"Relative pronouns are a type of word that introduces a subordinate relative sentence within the main one, as I explained before. That is, we use relative sentences to explain or modify something or someone by including another conjugated verb after the pronoun. We can find these words within the subject of a sentence or in structures like DO and IO, among others."

I then said these examples out loud:

- *La mujer **que** amo se llama Lorena* ("The woman I love is called Lorena")

- ***Quienes** saben español son muy inteligentes* ("Those who know Spanish are very smart")

- *Ella es la mujer **cuyo** hijo fue al espacio* ("She's the woman whose son went to space")

- *Te presentaré **cuantas** mujeres quieras* ("I will introduce you to as many women as you want")

- ***Quien** no conoce a Dios a cualquier santo le reza* ("Whoever doesn't know God will pray to any saint." This saying was Paula's idea).

Constructions with Relative Pronouns plus Prepositions

"¡Muy bien, George!" said Paula with a proud smile after hearing my explanation. "However, there is more to it than what you just said."

When she was about to go on, our drinks arrived, so we got distracted enjoying them and talking about how good they were. After a couple of minutes, Paula continued with her explanation related to constructions with relative pronouns:

"***Que, quien, quienes, cuanto, cuanta, cuantos, cuantas, cuyo, cuya, cuyos*** and ***cuyas*** are simple relative pronouns, and some of them need to be in agreement in gender and number with the noun they modify. Apart from these words, we have complex relatives to focus on. They are called complex because we need more than one word to use them. The structure includes a **definite article** (*el, la, los, las,* depending on the subject's gender and number), plus the words *que* or *cual.* In order to use them, we need to introduce them with a preposition."

These are some examples Paula gave me:

- *Esta es la chica **de la cual** te hablé* ("This is the girl I told you about")
- *¿Dónde era el lugar **en el que** comimos sushi?* ("Where was the place where we ate sushi?")
- *Encontré la valija **con la que** viajé a Suiza* ("I found the suitcase with which I traveled to Switzerland")
- *¡Esa es la fiesta **a la que** quiero invitarte!* ("That's the party I want to invite you to!")

Que / El que / El cual

As I understood it, *que* can be used on its own or with a definite article and can modify practically anything – whether a person, an object, an event, or even an abstract idea. According to Paula, we cannot use *que* on its own after a preposition: we can only include these *preposiciones* when we use a complex relative like *el que:*

- *El hombre con que salí X*
- *El hombre **con el que** salí* ✓

Then, if I wanted to use *el que, la que, los que* or *las que* without a preposition before them, Paula said this relative clause should be between commas, and it's a great way of explaining which subject we are referring to when there is confusion. For example, if I wanted to talk about one of Paula's brothers, I should explain which of the two brothers I'm referring to:

- *El hermano de Paula, **el que** se llama Carlos, es médico.*

An easier way of saying this would be *El hermano de Paula, Carlos, es médico.* Of course, the definite article you use can change the meaning of the sentence:

- *El hermano de Paula, **la que** viajó conmigo a México, es genial* (I'm talking about Paula here, not Carlos)

Paula also clarified that the relative pronoun *cual* can only appear before *el, la, los,* or *las.* These complex relatives are basically equivalents of el que, la que, los que, and *las que,* and we can use them as an alternative, although the variants with *cual* are a bit more formal. If we are going to directly specify with a relative pronoun (that is, without using a sentence between commas), we have to include a preposition:

- *La escuela a cual fui X*

- *La escuela **a la cual** fui* ✓

However, if we want to explain a subject by using a subordinate sentence (between commas), we can use the relatives with or without a preposition:

- *Morena, **la cual** conocí en una fiesta, tiene 30 años* ("Morena, who I met at a party, is 30 years old")

- *Morena, **con la cual** bailé el sábado, tiene 30 años* ("Morena, with whom I danced on Saturday, is 30 years old")

Lo que / Lo cual

These two complex relatives don't refer to a single subject, but to a previous sentence or situation, as in *María quiere saber **lo que** ocurrió ayer* ("María wants to know what happened yesterday"), or in *Falté al trabajo sin avisar, **lo que** me causará problemas* ("I have missed work without notice, which will cause me problems"). We mentioned these structures on Wednesday when Paula taught me about the neutral pronoun *lo.*

Quien

Quien or *quienes* are relatives used only to describe people and they can replace *que* or *cual* sometimes:

- *Es ella **a quien** conocí el otro día* ("She's the one I met the other day")

- *Meg, **con quien** estuve en pareja hace 5 años, hoy tuvo un hijo* ("Meg, with whom I was in a couple 5 years ago, had a son today")

- *Tobías, **quien** tiene un hermano gemelo, es un gran amigo* ("Tobías, who has a twin brother, is a great friend")

- ***Quien** come callado, come dos veces* ("Whoever eats quietly, eats twice." This was a saying Paula told me)

Cuyo, cuya, cuyos, cuyas

Then, Paula told me that this type of relative adds information about possession. One key thing is that these words must be in agreement in gender and number with the possessed person or object, not the possessor:

- *Mi amiga, **cuyo** perro se llama Pupi, también tiene un loro* ("My friend, whose dog is called Pupi, also has a parrot")
- *Es un hombre **cuyos** hijos se exiliaron hace un año* ("He's a man whose children went into exile a year ago")

Cuanto, cuanta, cuantos, cuantas

On a different note, Paula told me these relative pronouns refer to quantity and can be replaced by the constructions *todo/a/os/as lo... que.* For example:

- *Vengan **cuantos** quieran / Vengan **todos los que** quieran* ("Come as many as you want")

Constructions with Relative Adverbs plus Prepositions

- *Quiero volver **por donde** vinimos* ("I want to go back the way we came from")
- *Pueden quedarse despiertos **hasta cuando** quieran* ("They can stay up as long as they want")
- *Ellos corren **hasta donde** empieza el mar* ("They run to where the sea begins")

Night had arrived, and rain was still pouring down, so we decided to have dinner right there, in the hotel's *bistro.* Since we couldn't go out, we thought it would be a good idea to really spoil ourselves with a nice bottle of wine and a delicious local dish: the *fiambre estilo San Miguel de Allende,* a mixture of various meats, fruit, vegetables, and seeds, all dipped in a vinaigrette and served on a bed of lettuce.

Mexican Cultural Annex

While we were having dinner, Paula grabbed her phone and looked up the story of San Miguel de Allende on its official website. She read it to me so I could practice my Spanish:

En 1542, el Fray Juan de San Miguel, fundó este asentamiento bajo el nombre de San Miguel el Grande. Este era un punto estratégico para el virreinato español, ya que pertenecía a la ruta de la plata, metal precioso que abundaba en la región. "San Miguel de Allende" se instauró en 1826, cuando el poblado consiguió su estatus de ciudad. El nombre actual se creó gracias a la combinación de dos nombres: el Fray Juan de San Miguel e Ignacio José de Allende y Unzaga, una figura destacada de la independencia de México.

Esta ciudad dejó de estar dominada por España durante la guerra de Independencia. Ignacio Allende estuvo a la cabeza de la resistencia hasta ser capturado por los realistas, quienes lo sentenciaron a muerte. Tras ser fusilado, el líder independentista se consagró como mártir y héroe nacional.

Ya en los inicios del siglo XX, San Miguel de Allende, una ciudad cuyo corazón productivo giraba en torno a la minería, sufrió el abandono de su población, ya que las minas perdieron su popularidad. A riesgo de convertirse en un pueblo fantasma, el gobierno mexicano intercedió y declaró a la ciudad Monumento Histórico para conservar el atractivo de la ciudad. Afortunadamente, a mediados de siglo San Miguel de Allende volvió a poblarse y recobró su atractivo colonial.

Chapter Summary

After a lovely day of Spanish learning and Mexican adventures, I did a small recap before I went to bed:

- First of all, Paula helped me remember how reflexive verbs worked, as well as how to use them with modal verbs and in the imperative mood.

- Then, we saw how to use the word *se* to make passive-voice sentences.

- We also learned another type of passive voice sentence, one that requires the verb *estar*.

- Finally, we focused on the morphology and uses of relative adverbs and pronouns like *que, el cual, donde*, etc., and saw how we could pair them up with different prepositions when using relative clauses.

Exercises

1. Come up with one example sentence for each verb combination:
   a. *afeitarse - poder*
   b. *irse - querer*
   c. *maquillarse - soler*
   d. *ducharse - necesitar*

2. Translate the following sentences with reflexive verbs in the imperative mood:
   a. "Get down from that tree, children!"
   b. "Stay here, I'll be right back."
   c. "Guys, let's put some makeup on before the show."

3. Decide whether the following statements are true or false. If false, correct them.
   a. The relative pronoun *quien* is only used to refer to an object, not a person.
   b. The passive voice phrase *Los platos están suciados* is correct.

4. Decide whether the following sentences are right or wrong. Correct the wrong ones.

   a. *Es una mujer cuya esposo se llama Lorenzo.*

   b. *Eso era lo que quería decirte.*

   c. *Aquella muchacha de que me enamoré.*

5. Translate the following sentences with *estar*:
   a. "The door was open when I arrived."
   b. "Is your money kept in the bank?"
   c. "Is your home insured?"

6. *Sábado: Palabras difíciles*

When I woke up that quiet Friday morning, I was happily surprised to see that the rain had completely disappeared and that a few rays of sunshine were piercing through the hotel room's blinds. This was excellent news: we only had 2 days left of our trip, so we had to enjoy Mexico as much as possible!

Uses of *se*

We started our morning in the Jardín Allende, the city's main square – across the street from the parish we had seen the day before. Thankfully, the sun was shining brightly in the sky, so the streets were really crowded, with children enjoying their weekend off. This joyful morning was the perfect time to begin my Spanish lesson.

During my time studying this awesome language, I learned that *se* has a lot of different meanings and uses. The first distinction Paula made was between *se* and *sé* (with an accent mark).

Sé

Sé with an accent mark is a conjugation of the verbs *saber* ("to know") and *ser* ("to be"). Of course, my friend gave some examples:

- ***Sé** que el español es complejo, pero quiero aprenderlo igual* ("I know Spanish is complex, but I want to study it anyway").
- ***Sé** bueno y tráeme un vaso de agua* ("Be a good boy and bring me a glass of water").

Se as an invariable personal pronoun replacing *le* and *les*

I had seen one of these uses of *se* when revising my notes on the plane - and again on Wednesday when Paula explained the direct and indirect objects. *Se* replaces *le* and *les* when they are used as an indirect object pronoun and come before *lo, los, la,* or *las.* Paula gave some examples so that I could really grasp this use of *se*:

- *Le pedí una cerveza al mozo* ("I ordered a beer from the waiter").

becomes

- *Se la pedí al mozo* ("I ordered it from the waiter").

Another example:

- *Les llevo estos regalos a mis amigos* ("I'm bringing these presents for my friends").

becomes

- *Se los llevo a mis amigos* ("I'm bringing them for my friends").

Se as a third-person personal pronoun

After strolling around the square, we decided to visit Casa Museo Allende, a museum dedicated to Ignacio de Allende y Unzaga, Mexican independence leader and hero. He was born and raised in that very building during the second half of the eighteenth century. Its harmonious mixture of baroque and neoclassical styles was evident in the building's front, as our tour guide told us, with small balconies and a statue of Allende himself right in the middle of the corner (the house was located at an intersection.)

As we toured the inside of the building, Paula continued with her explanation. From what I understood, another use of *se* is as a third-person personal pronoun with reflexive or reciprocal value, with reflexive verbs, which we saw on Friday. *Se* can indicate that the subject performs the action on themselves or orders it to be performed on themselves (reflexive) or that the action is performed by several individuals, one on another (reciprocal). These are the examples Paula gave me:

- *Carlos se viste bien* ("Carlos dresses well").
- *Antes de comer, los niños se lavan las manos* ("Before eating, the children wash their hands").

- *El novio y la novia **se** besaron en el altar* ("The groom and the bride kissed at the altar").

Paula said that *se* is used in these examples because the subject is in the third person. If we changed the subject of the previous sentences, the pronoun would also change. For example.

- *Antes de comer, **me** lavo las manos* ("Before eating, I wash my hands").

Another use of *se* is as a third-person personal pronoun with expressive value. This is another reflexive use of *se*; that is, it refers to the subject of the sentence. Its syntactic function is similar to that of the indirect object, but it's not required by the verb. Its presence provides expressive nuances, and it can be deleted without changing its meaning. These are some examples:

- *Nico **(se)** comió tres platos de pasta* ("Nico ate three pasta dishes").
- *Micaela **(se)** leyó todo el diccionario* ("Micaela read the whole dictionary").

Again, in this case, *se* is used because the subject is in the third person, but we could say:

- *Nosotras **(nos)** comimos tres platos de pasta* ("We ate three pasta dishes").

Se as a component of the third person forms of pronominal verbs

As we visited the different rooms in the Casa Museo Allende, Paula told me that there was a replica of a *pulpería*, a commercial and social establishment that exists throughout Latin America. There, people could buy food and supplies such as candles, fabrics, etc., but it was also a gathering point for the popular and middle classes, a place where they could discuss the news of the day while sharing a drink, playing guitar, or playing cards, for example.

Paula, who wished to continue with her explanation of *se*, told me there are other verbs that don't have a reflexive meaning but are constructed in all their forms with an unstressed reflexive pronoun, which plays no syntactic role in the sentence. The form that corresponds to the third persons, the second person plural, and the formal second person is *se*:

- *Él **se** arrepiente de lo que hizo ("He regrets what he did").*

- *Ellas **se** adueñaron de la casa ("They took possession of the house").*

- *Usted **se** queja mucho ("You complain a lot").*

Se as an indicator of impersonal sentences or of reflexive passive voice

Throughout my trip, I had learned about the passive voice and impersonal sentences, so this was just a revision.

Se is used in impersonal sentences, the ones that have no subject. *Se* comes before the verbs conjugated in the third person singular:

- *En México **se** come muy bien* ("The food in Mexico is very good").

- *En el sur de Estados Unidos **se** habla mucho español* ("In the south of the United States, Spanish is spoken a lot").

When the impersonal sentence has a plural direct object, the verb shouldn't be in the plural, since the number agreement only occurs between the verb and the subject, not between the verb and the object:

- *En el cumpleaños, **se** comió tacos, pizzas y nachos* ("On the birthday, tacos, pizza and nachos were eaten").

In reflexive passive sentences, *se* is preceded by a verb in the active form in the third person (singular or plural), next to a nominal element, which is usually postponed and functions as its grammatical subject. This nominal element usually denotes undetermined people, things, or actions. This is the case for the summer house for sale that we saw on Friday. These are some more examples that Paula gave me:

- ***Se** vende fruta fresca* ("Fresh fruit is sold").

- *En la reunión **se** discutieron temas importantes* ("Important topics were discussed at the meeting").

"Oh, *se* has so many uses," I told Paula when we were done with this short but polysemic word.

"That's because we haven't talked about *que* in detail yet," said Paula.

Uses of *que*

When we finished visiting the museum about Ignacio de Allende, we had to stop to have lunch. We took the opportunity to try some delicious local food; since it was a hot day, we ordered some nieves de tuna, a popular dessert which consists of a *tuna* (a cactus also known as *nopal*) made into ice-cream. I was a little skeptical about eating a cactus, to be honest, but it ended up being really sweet and refreshing.

After asking for the check, the woman who had been our waiter recommended that we go to the Mercado de Artesanías, a craft market eight blocks from where we were sitting at the time. As we walked to our destination, Paula decided to explain the different uses of the word *que* in Spanish.

"Again, the first distinction we need to make is between *que* and *qué*," she said.

Qué

What I understood from Paula's explanation is that *qué* with an accent mark has an interrogative or exclamatory meaning.

It can be an equivalent of "what":

- *¿**Qué** aprendiste hoy?* ("What did you learn today?").
- *¡**Qué** país extraordinario es México!* ("What an extraordinary country Mexico is!").

It can also mean "which":

- *¿**Qué** libro usas para aprender español?* ("Which book do you use to learn Spanish?").
- *¿**Qué** habitación prefieres?* ("Which room do you prefer?").

And finally, *qué* can also function as an adverb, and it means "how":

- *¡**Qué** rico este taco!* ("How delicious this taco is!").
- *¡Con **qué** claridad explica Paula!* ("How clearly Paula explains!").

All the examples Paula had given me about *qué* had question or exclamation marks, so I told her that it wasn't so difficult to distinguish *qué* from *que*; you only needed to see if there were any question or exclamation marks!

"It's not so simple, George," she said. "There are cases where *qué* has an interrogative or exclamatory meaning outside a question or an exclamation. And there are also cases where *que* has other meanings, but it appears inside a question or an exclamation." And, of course, she gave some examples:

*No sé **qué** quieres hacer tú, pero yo quiero ir a dormir* ("I don't know what you want to do, but I want to go to bed").

- *¿Conoces a alguien **que** enseñe español?* ("Do you know anyone who teaches Spanish?").

Que

Que without an accent mark can function as a relative pronoun or as a conjunction.

Most of the time, it means "that":

- *El país **que** más quiero visitar es México* ("The country that I want to visit the most is Mexico").
- *Mi hermana **que** vive en Nueva York tiene dos hijos* ("My sister who lives in New York has two children").

It can also mean "which," "who" or "whom":

- *Mi otra hermana, **que** no tiene hijos, vive en Chicago* ("My other sister, who doesn't have children, lives in Chicago").
- *Nadie usaba la silla roja, **que** era incómoda* ("No one used the red chair, which was uncomfortable").
- *La chica con la **que** compartí el taxi era mexicana* ("The girl with whom I shared a taxi was Mexican").

In comparisons, it can mean "than" or "to":

- *En este viaje he aprendido más **que** en los anteriores* ("In this trip I have learn more than in the previous ones").
- *Prefiero tacos **que** burritos* ("I prefer tacos to burritos").

In the periphrasis *tener que* ("to have to"), it also means "to":

- Tengo **que** hacer el check out del hotel ("I have to check out of my hotel").

In some set phrases, *que* means "may":

- ***Que** descanse en paz* ("May she rest in peace").
- ***Que** Dios los bendiga* ("May God bless you").

When Paula finished explaining all the uses of *que*, she told me that I shouldn't be overwhelmed since I already knew and used most of them. And, when I started paying attention, I realized that it was true – which makes sense since *que* is the third most used word in Spanish (according to the internet, at least.)

Hasta

When we arrived at the Mercado de Artesanías, I was surprised by how colorful it was! Its long and narrow halls displayed many Mexican openwork paper garlands hanging from the ceiling, with popular designs from the country's culture. On each side, we could see shops with different types of crafts: knitted items of clothing, woven baskets, embroidered tablecloths and dresses, jewelry and metalwork, traditional hats, pocket mirrors... The list went on and on, and the items were so different from those offered in the markets back in Los Angeles.

As we looked around, Paula suggested we move on to prepositions. Paula told me that, even though *hasta* seems like a pretty plain word, it can be tricky, especially in Mexico! So, she explained the different meanings and uses of *hasta*.

Hasta for limits

We use *hasta* to indicate a limit in time. In this case, it can be translated as "up to" or "until":

- *Voy a estar en México **hasta** el domingo* ("I'm going to be in Mexico until Sunday").

- *Paula me enseñó español **hasta** el último minuto* ("Paula taught me Spanish up to the very last minute").

- *No empezaré a comer **hasta** que llegue Paula* ("I won't start eating until Paula arrives").

We use *hasta* for limits in space, and we translate it as "up to" or "to."

- *Caminé **hasta** el taxi y le pregunté al chofer si estaba disponible* ("I walked up to the taxi and asked the driver if he was available").

- *Tienes que ir **hasta** la avenida principal y doblar a la izquierda* ("You have to go to the main avenue and turn left").

We also use it for numerical limits. In this case, it means "up to."

- *En la habitación pueden dormir **hasta** cuatro personas* ("Up to four people can sleep in the room").

- *Un pasaje a México puede costar **hasta** mil dólares* ("A ticket to Mexico can cost up to a thousand dollars").

Emphatic use of *hasta*

There's also an emphatic use of *hasta*, which can be translated as "even":

- **Hasta** *la vecina se quejó del ruido* ("Even our neighbor complained about the noise").

- **Hasta** *el arroz es picante en México* ("Even rice is spicy in Mexico").

Hasta in set phrases

Finally, there are some set phrases where we can find the preposition *hasta*:

- *estar* **hasta** *la coronilla* ("to be fed up").

- *hasta luego,* **hasta** *pronto,* **hasta** *mañana,* **hasta** *la próxima* ("see you later, see you soon, see you tomorrow, see you next time").

- **hasta** *nunca* ("see you never").

Por and *para*

As it was getting dark, Paula told me that a famous summer festival from San Miguel de Allende was taking place that week. It was called the Festival Internacional de Música de Cámara ("San Miguel de Allende Chamber Music Festival"), and each summer, it gathers musicians (and music lovers in general) to enjoy concerts in different parts of the city – in places that don't normally host this type of events, such as churches. A couple of kilometers away from where we were at the time, a jazz concert was about to begin, so we went back to the hotel to get the car and drove there.

On the way over, Paula wanted to finish our review of difficult words, so we talked about a pair of confusing prepositions. *Por* and *para* are two Spanish prepositions that, even though they mean the same in English ("for"), each one has its own specific contexts of use. Many advanced students keep mixing them up after years of practice, so don't feel bad if you do, too! Let's see when we have to use each one:

Por

First of all, we use *por* when we want to express **cause**, the reason why we do something. For example, if you are watching a TV show about a murder and the detective asks the culprit why he killed the victim, he might say the following sentences:

- *Lo maté por dinero* ("I killed him for money")
- *Lo hice por envidia* ("I did it out of envy")
- *Lo hice por celos* ("I did it out of jealousy")
- *Lo maté por diversión* ("I killed him for fun")

"As you may have noticed," said Paula, "every word that comes after *por* is a noun; however, if we wanted to continue our phrase with another verb or with a more complex explanation, we are going to use the word *porque*."

- *Lo maté porque me debía dinero* ("I killed him because he owed me money")
- *Lo hice porque envidiaba su vida* ("I did it because I envied his life")
- *Lo hice porque sentía celos por él* ("I did it because I was jealous of him")
- *Lo maté porque me divertía la idea* ("I killed him because the idea amused me")

Then, Paula told me the preposition *por* is used when describing **movement** in space, that is, walking through a place or location. Here, we wouldn't translate *por* as "for," but as "through." For example:

- *Este es nuestro tercer viaje por México* ("This is our third trip through Mexico")
- *Ahora estamos caminando por Guanajuato* ("Right now, we are walking through Guanajuato")
- *Ayer, también estuvimos paseando por Guanajuato* ("Yesterday, we were also strolling around Guanajuato")

We can also use *por* to talk about a specific **duration** of an action. You can recognize this type of context because it works as the answer for the question "For how long?":

- *Nos fuimos de vacaciones por una semana* ("We went on vacations for one week")
- *¡Ayer caminamos por cinco horas!* ("Yesterday we walked for five hours!")
- *Puedo aguantar la respiración por 40 segundos* ("I can hold my breath for 40 seconds")

Regarding time, we can describe a specific **moment** of the day by using *por*. In other words, *por* describes the moment of the day during which an action takes place (especially if we are talking about habits or routines). You could translate *por* as "in" and, in most cases, it can be replaced by the preposition *a*:

- *Nosotros nos duchamos **por** la mañana* ("We took a shower in the morning")
- *¿Sueles dormir la siesta **por** la tarde?* (Do you usually take a nap in the afternoon?)
- *No como comida frita **por** las noches* ("I don't eat fried food at night")

Then, one may find *por* when talking about a **medium**, that is, the channel by which we do something, and we would use the English words "via" or "on" to translate this preposition. In some cases, *por* can be replaced by the preposition *en:*

- *Compré mis billetes de avión **por** Internet* ("I bought my plane tickets on the Internet")
- *Hablamos **por** teléfono bastante seguido* ("We talk on the phone quite often")
- *¡Te envío la dirección **por** mensaje!* ("I'll send you the address via text!")

Finally, we have the preposition *por* to talk about **price** and exchange of goods. A good rule of thumb is that whenever you want to talk about numbers, you are going to need *por:*

- *Compramos un refresco **por** 25 pesos* ("We bought a soda for 25 pesos")
- *Cambié mi vestido nuevo **por** unos pantalones* ("I exchanged my new dress for a pair of pants")
- *¿Cuánto **por** ese sombrero?* ("How much for that hat?")

In summary, these are the uses that *por* has in a sentence:

- to express cause
- to describe movement
- to talk about duration
- to describe a moment in the day
- to highlight a medium
- and to talk about price or exchange

Para

Para also has many uses for us Spanish speakers. For starters, it can indicate the **purpose**, goal, or objective of an action and why we do the things we do. It can be translated by using the preposition "to," and you will always find <u>a verb in its bare form</u> after *para:*

- *Tú viajas a México **para** mejorar tu español* ("You travel to Mexico to improve your Spanish")

- *Nosotros salimos del hotel temprano **para** visitar más lugares* ("We left the hotel early to visit more places")

- *Comemos comida grasosa **para** ser más felices* ("We eat greasy food to be happier")

Second of all, you can find *para* in sentences related to **destination**, that is, where we are going. We can also use the Spanish preposition *a:*

- *Mañana viajamos **para** Querétaro* ("Tomorrow we travel to Querétaro")

- *El domingo vuelves **para** Estados Unidos* ("On Sunday, you go back to the United States")

- *Estamos yendo **para** allá* ("We're on our way there")

In third place, *para* is used to mark time limits or **deadlines**, and it can be translated as "by":

- *Tienes que aprender este tema **para** mañana* ("You need to learn this topic by tomorrow")

- *Terminaré de empacar **para** el domingo* ("I will finish packing by Sunday")

- *¿Puedes terminar el informe **para** mañana?* ("Can you finish the report by tomorrow?")

Then, we can use *para* to talk about the *destinatario,* that is, the **recipient** or receiver of our action:

- *Estoy escribiendo un correo **para** mi madre* ("I'm writing an email for my mom")

- *Este plato no es **para** mí, es **para** ella* ("This dish is not for me, it is for her")

- *¿Tienes un regalo **para** mí?* ("Do you have a present for me?")

Finally, we can find *para* in sentences that express an **opinion** or a subjective assessment:

- *Este clima es demasiado caluroso **para** ti* ("This weather is too hot for you")
- ***Para** nosotros, este lugar es más bonito que el anterior* ("For us, this place is prettier than the last one")
- ***Para** mí, México es un país hermoso* ("For me, Mexico is a beautiful country")

After Paula's explanation, I understood everything... Well, almost everything. I was still a bit confused about the difference between *por* and *para* when talking about a cause or a purpose. As a solution, Paula gave me a set of phrases to compare these prepositions:

- *Trabajé **por** mi padre* (I worked for him, to help him pay rent).
- *Trabajé **para** mi padre* (I was my dad's employee).

In summary, these are the uses that *para* has in a sentence:

- to indicate purpose
- to state destination
- to mark deadlines
- to talk about the recipient of an action
- and to express an opinion

And with that, Paula finished her lesson on difficult Spanish words, just in time for the show to begin! It was a beautiful and magical evening.

Mexican Cultural Annex

On our way back to our hotel, for our traditional cultural bit, Paula told me about another meaning of *hasta*, which is mostly used in Mexico, Central America, and some regions of Ecuador and Colombia. In these places, *hasta* means "not before." She gave this example:

- *Llegaré a casa **hasta** la noche* ("I won't be home before evening").

This use can be quite confusing since it means exactly the opposite of the first meaning of *hasta* we saw, the one that's equivalent to "until." Check this sentence:

- *Los pasajeros pueden embarcar **hasta** una hora antes del despegue.*

If this was said outside of Mexico, we would translate it as:

- Passengers can board up to one hour before takeoff.

However, if we hear this phrase in Mexico, it could also mean:

- Passengers cannot board until one hour before takeoff.

I was pretty confused by this, but Paula gave me some advice:

"Whenever you hear *hasta* in Mexico, just double check with whoever said it to see if you got the correct meaning."

Chapter Summary

As always, before going to bed, I sat down and made a summary of the things I had learned:

- *Sé* is the first person singular of the present indicative of the verb *saber* and the second person singular of the imperative of the verb *ser*.
- *Se* can be a pronoun:
  - it replaces indirect object pronouns *le* and *les* when they come before *lo, los, la* or *las* to avoid cacophony.
  - with reflexive verbs, it has reflexive or reciprocal value.
  - it can be a component of the third-person forms of pronominal verbs
- *Se* is used in impersonal sentences.
- *Se* is also used in reflexive passive sentences.
- *Qué* has an interrogative or exclamatory meaning, and it can mean: "what," "which," and "how."
- *Que* as a relative pronoun means: "that," "which," "who," and "whom."
- *Que* as also appears:
  - in comparisons, meaning "that" or "to."
  - in the periphrasis *tener que*, meaning "to."
  - in set phrases, meaning "may."
- When *hasta* denotes a time limit, it can be translated as "up to" or "until."
- When *hasta* is used to denote a limit in space, it can be translated as "up to" or "to."
- When we use *hasta* for numerical limits, it also means "up to."
- *Hasta* has an emphatic use, similar to the English "even."

- *Hasta* is used in set phrases, such as *hasta mañana, estar hasta la coronilla* and *hasta nunca*.
- In Mexico and other Latin American regions, *hasta* also means "not before," which can be a bit confusing.
- Both *por* and *para* mean "for," but each one has its own uses.
  - *Por* is used to:
    - express cause
    - describe movement
    - talk about duration
    - describe a moment in the day
    - highlight a medium
    - talk about a price
  - *Para* is used to:
    - indicate purpose
    - state a destination
    - mark a deadline
    - talk about the recipient of an action
    - express an opinion

Exercises

1. Complete the following sentences using *sé* or *se*.
   a. *No me pidas que cocine, no _____ hacerlo.*
   b. *_____ busca profesora de español.*
   c. *Mi abuela _____ lava el pelo en la peluquería.*
   d. *¡_____ obediente y haz lo que te dice tu madre!*
   e. *Compré chocolates en el freeshop y _____ los regalé a una amiga.*

2. Complete the following sentences using *qué* or *que*.
   a. *Este año gané menos dinero _____ el año pasado.*
   b. *Mi hermana, _____ no pudo venir, te manda un cariño.*
   c. *No entiendo por _____ aún no han llegado los demás.*

d. *Los pasajeros _____ lleguen tarde no podrán abordar el avión.*

e. *¡_____ casa más bonita!*

3. Decide whether the following sentences are right or wrong. Correct the wrong ones.

   a. *Compré mucha salsa picante. Le la llevo de regalo a mi padre.*

   b. *Ahora entiendo por que dicen que México es tan lindo.*

   c. *Qué vista más linda.*

   d. *En el carro entran para cuatro pasajeros.*

   e. *Tuve que apurarme para no perder el avión.*

4. Match each word on the left with a possible translation on the right.

   a. *qué*   1. may

   b. *hasta*   2. know

   c. *por*   3. nor before

   d. *sé*   4. what

   e. *que*   5. for

5. Complete the following sentences using *por, porque* or *para*.

   a. *Vine a México _____ visitar a mi amiga Paula.*

   b. *También vine _____ quería aprender español.*

   c. *En su primer viaje, George estuvo en México _____ una semana.*

   d. *Siempre que viajo, llevo regalos _____ mi familia.*

   e. *Si no te atienden _____ teléfono, prueba hacerlo _____ internet.*

7. Domingo: ¡Nos vemos!

Finally, the time had come; it was our last day in San Miguel de Allende for Paula and me and my last day in Mexico, a country that had brought me so much joy and still does to this day. Paula told me she had a surprise in store for us but that I would find out what it was after breakfast. Once our bellies were full, we hopped in the car and drove around for a bit before we got to our destination.

I couldn't believe my eyes: six massive hot air balloons hovered lightly near the ground, held in place by sandbags and ropes to keep them from flying away. The colors were vibrant and formed a beautiful composition of patterns. Some balloons had geometric shapes, others had plants and animals, and the rest had stars. I hadn't been in the air many times, only on my flights to México, let alone on a hot air balloon.

"*¿Qué piensas?*" asked Paula.

"*¡Es increíble!*" I replied with a smile as big as my excitement.

I felt a little vertigo once we were in the air: I didn't know I was so afraid of heights! The view was breathtaking, but I couldn't really look down because I was afraid of falling or something. To keep me from having a minor anxiety attack, Paula decided to teach me some Spanish tips that would distract me for a while.

Reading Comprehension Strategies

I was so afraid of falling out of the balloon that I paid close attention to everything Paula told me. She wanted to give me tips for when I had to have a long Spanish text on my own, whether it was a novel, a description at an art gallery, or something else. She organized the different strategies into three categories:

1) Global strategies

- Focus on the **communicative context** of the text.
  - Who is the author?
  - Where was it published? Was it a newspaper?
  - Who is the text talking to?
  - What is the main message?
- Establish the **purpose/objective** of the text.
  - Does it want to inform?
  - Does it want to sell something?
  - Does it want to make you laugh?
- Identify how the text is **organized.**
  - Is it divided into sections?
  - Can you identify any subheadings?
- Train your directed or **selective attention.**
  - What is the main information I need to focus on?
  - What can I ignore on the first reading and then go back?
- Use the information provided by **paratextual elements.**
  - Does it have any pictures?
  - Does the text include a graph or a chart?
- Identify **key information** given by the text.
  - Can you spot any words in bold or italics?

2) Conflict resolution strategies

- **Go back** to the text as many times as necessary.
- Adjust the **reading speed** depending on the text.
- **Pause** and think about what you are reading.
- Imagine or **visualize** the information in your head.
- **Reread** complex parts of the text.
- **Use context** to understand unfamiliar words or phrases.

- Identify cognates or **transparent words** (i.e., words that share a similar spelling across languages or that come from the same root, such as Latin).
- Recognize **previous references** by focusing on pronouns.

3) Support strategies
- **Take notes** while reading.
- **Read aloud** difficult words or phrases you encounter.
- **Paraphrase** what you read.
- **Underline**, circle, or highlight key information.

After Paula's explanation, I was able to calm my nerves down for a bit, and I dared take a peek below. We were so high up that I could hardly see people on the streets, only cars, which looked like little dots moving and turning. That distance helped me put everything into perspective: My Spanish journey had started not so long ago, and yet I felt as if I had been learning that language for many, many years. It was as if Mexico, with its beautiful landscapes and passionate people, had been helping me on my learning curve for all that time. As I was having this realization, I turned my head to face Paula and saw the look of pride in my friend's eyes: she could see me getting emotional, and that struck a chord with her as well.

In that state of mind and feeling so moved, both by the emotional part and by the swaying of the hot air balloon, we embraced each other as we gazed at the streets of San Miguel de Allende from a distance.

Writing tips

When the ride was over, it was time to grab some lunch, but we had to wait for a little bit until my nerves calmed down completely. Then, we decided to walk one kilometer to reach a place called El Charco del Ingenio Botanical Garden, which could be literally translated as "The pool of wit." This nature reserve was apparently packed with a large collection of cacti and native flora, including endangered plants, so we really wanted to check it out.

Once there, we were greeted by a cornucopia of native plants with ripe fruits and blooming flowers all around. However, the local fauna was designed for a dry biosphere, so it was more incredible to find huge cacti a couple of meters tall! As we explored the grounds, Paula thought it would be a good idea to give me a couple of tips so I could feel confident about writing.

"I know we usually talk, not write," said Paula, "but I want you to be ready if you want to engage in anything related to writing, either during your personal time or at work."

These are the notes I took with Paula's useful writing tips:

- Think about the **key message** you want to communicate.
  - What keywords have to be included in order to express yourself correctly?
- Think about the **potential reader.**
  - Is it someone who has previous knowledge of what you are talking about?
  - In what register should you write to be respectful and/or to capture their attention?
- Think about the **effect** you want to produce on the reader.
  - Do you want to inform them, entice them, or make them laugh?
  - What is the best strategy to accomplish that?
- Before writing, make a **detailed outline** of everything you want to include.
  - How can you organize your information?
  - How many paragraphs will your text need?
  - Should you include an introduction and a conclusion?
- Write in **simple sentences** and try to translate from English as little as possible.
  - Is there a way to say that sentence more clearly and directly?
  - Are there false friends you should be worried about or words that you usually confuse?
- If you have the opportunity, ask a **native speaker** to take a look at your text.
  - Is there anything in your text that might sound more natural to a native speaker?
  - Would regionalisms add more vibrancy to your text?
  - If that's the case, which ones can you use?

Mexican Cultural Annex

After our walk, it was time to return to the hotel to pack and drive to Guanajuato, where my flight was leaving. On our way to the airport, Paula told me about one writer from San Miguel de Allende I could read with my reading comprehension tips.

She was talking about **Ignacio Ramírez "El Nigromante."** He was a poet, journalist, lawyer, politician, and thinker who lived during the time of Mexico's independence, and he made great contributions to secularism within the government. He was known as the Mexican Voltaire. For his will to reform the state politically, economically, and religiously to make it more liberal, he was briefly imprisoned but later became President of the Supreme Court of Justice.

"In general, San Miguel de Allende is a city that struck a chord with many literary artists of the twentieth century," said Paula. "For example, the literary movement known as the Beat Generation saw this city as their favorite destination within Mexico. It's a well-known fact that Jack Kerouac, William Burroughs, and Neal Cassady walked these very streets!"

Chapter Summary

After an hour or so, we arrived at the airport. My flight was about to leave, so we decided to review what we had learned as we stood in line for check-in:

- We looked at some reading comprehension tips, which consisted of focusing on the context, purpose, main message, and structure of the text, among other things.
- Then, Paula taught me some writing strategies that involved focusing on the key message and the potential reader, plus making a detailed outline of the text (among other important things).

Exercises

1. Read the short story *"El huesped"* (1959) by Mexican writer Amparo Dávila. Remember to put the reading comprehension tips into action to really grasp the meaning of the text. You will find the bolded words translated in a glossary at the end of the

story.

2. Read the short story again and determine whether the following statements are true or false. Justify your answer using a quote from the short story when possible.

    a. *La narradora está felizmente casada.*

    b. *La familia vive en un pueblo alejado de la ciudad.*

    c. *La criatura que lleva el marido a vivir en la casa es un perro.*

    d. *Guadalupe es la empleada doméstica.*

    e. *En total, viven tres niños en la casa.*

3. Now, answer the following reading comprehension questions:

    a. *¿Cómo era el cuarto en el que vivía la criatura?*

    b. *¿Qué le gustaba hacer por las tardes a la narradora?*

    c. *¿Quién es Martín?*

    d. *¿Por qué la narradora no huye de la casa?*

    e. *¿Qué le dice la narradora a su marido sobre la muerte de la criatura?*

4. Write a detailed description of your hometown in 150 words or more. Describe the atmosphere one can feel when walking the streets of this place, the people who live there, the fauna and flora one could find, what smells are usually present, or what sounds one may be able to hear during the day or at night. Be as thorough as you can and try to incorporate many adjectives and specific vocabulary.

5. Tell an anecdote from your childhood in 150 words or more. Use a first-person narrator and include the following information:

- When and where was this?

- Who were you with? What bond did you have with this person/these people?

- What was the main problem/conflict of your anecdote?

- How did you solve this problem/conflict?

Try to be as thorough as you can with your character description, and try to include your thoughts and feelings at the time.

El huésped

Nunca olvidaré el día en que vino a vivir con nosotros. Mi marido lo trajo al regreso de un viaje.

Llevábamos entonces cerca de tres años de matrimonio, teníamos dos niños y yo no era feliz. Representaba para mi marido algo así como un mueble, que se acostumbra uno a ver en determinado sitio, pero que no causa la menor impresión. Vivíamos en un pueblo pequeño, incomunicado y distante de la ciudad. Un pueblo casi muerto o a punto de desaparecer.

No pude **reprimir** un grito de horror, cuando lo vi por primera vez. Era lúgubre, siniestro. Con grandes ojos amarillentos, casi redondos y sin **parpadeo**, que parecían penetrar a través de las cosas y de las personas.

Mi vida **desdichada** se convirtió en un infierno. La misma noche de su llegada supliqué a mi marido que no me condenara a la tortura de su compañía. No podía resistirlo; me inspiraba desconfianza y horror. "Es completamente **inofensivo**", dijo mi marido mirándome con marcada indiferencia. "Te acostumbrarás a su compañía y, si no lo consigues..." No hubo manera de convencerlo de que se lo llevara. Se quedó en nuestra casa.

No fui la única en sufrir con su presencia. Todos los de la casa – mis niños, la mujer que me ayudaba en los **quehaceres**, su hijito – sentíamos **pavor** de él. Sólo mi marido **gozaba** teniéndolo allí.

Desde el primer día mi marido le asignó el cuarto de la esquina. Era ésta una **pieza** grande, pero húmeda y oscura. Por esos inconvenientes yo nunca la ocupaba. Sin embargo él pareció sentirse contento con la habitación. Como era bastante oscura, se acomodaba a sus necesidades. Dormía hasta el oscurecer y nunca supe a qué hora se acostaba.

Perdí la poca paz de que gozaba en la casona. Durante el día, todo marchaba con aparente normalidad. Yo me levantaba siempre muy temprano, vestía a los niños que ya estaban despiertos, les daba el desayuno y los entretenía mientras Guadalupe arreglaba la casa y salía a comprar el **mandado**.

La casa era muy grande, con un jardín en el centro y los cuartos distribuidos a su alrededor. Entre las piezas y el jardín había corredores que protegían las habitaciones del rigor de las lluvias y del viento que eran frecuentes. Tener arreglada una casa tan grande y cuidado el jardín, mi diaria ocupación de la mañana, era tarea dura. Pero yo amaba mi *jardín. Los corredores estaban cubiertos por* **enredaderas** *que* **floreaban** *casi todo el año. Recuerdo cuánto me gustaba, por las tardes, sentarme en uno de aquellos corredores a* **coser** *la ropa de los niños, entre el perfume de las* **madreselvas** *y de las buganvilias.*

En el jardín cultivaba crisantemos, **pensamientos,** *violetas de los Alpes, begonias y heliotropos. Mientras yo regaba las plantas, los niños se entretenían buscando* **gusanos** *entre las hojas. A veces pasaban horas, callados y muy atentos, tratando de coger las* **gotas** *de agua que se escapaban de la vieja* **manguera.**

Yo no podía dejar de mirar, de vez en cuando, hacia el cuarto de la esquina. Aunque pasaba todo el día durmiendo no podía confiarme. Hubo veces que, cuando estaba preparando la comida, veía de pronto su **sombra** *proyectándose sobre la* **estufa** *de* **leña.** *Lo sentía detrás de mí... yo* **arrojaba** *al suelo lo que tenía en las manos y salía de la cocina corriendo y gritando como una* **loca.** *Él volvía nuevamente a su cuarto, como si nada hubiera pasado.*

Creo que ignoraba por completo a Guadalupe, nunca se acercaba a ella ni la **perseguía.** *No así a los niños y a mí. A ellos los odiaba y a mí me* **acechaba** *siempre.*

Cuando salía de su cuarto comenzaba la más terrible **pesadilla** *que alguien pueda vivir. Se situaba siempre en un pequeño* **cenador,** *enfrente de la puerta de mi cuarto. Yo no salía más. Algunas veces, pensando que aún dormía, yo iba hacia la cocina por la* **merienda** *de los niños, de pronto lo descubría en algún oscuro* **rincón** *del corredor, bajo las enredaderas. "¡Allí está ya, Guadalupe!" gritaba desesperada.*

Guadalupe y yo nunca lo nombrábamos, nos parecía que al hacerlo **cobraba** *realidad aquel ser* **tenebroso.** *Siempre decíamos: – allí está, ya salió, está durmiendo, él, él, él...*

Solamente hacía dos comidas, una cuando se levantaba al anochecer y otra, tal vez, en la **madrugada** *antes de acostarse. Guadalupe era la encargada de llevarle la bandeja, puedo asegurar que la arrojaba dentro del cuarto pues la pobre mujer sufría el mismo terror que yo. Toda su alimentación se reducía a carne, no probaba nada más.*

Cuando los niños se dormían, Guadalupe me llevaba la cena al cuarto. Yo no podía dejarlos solos, sabiendo que se había levantado o estaba por hacerlo. Una vez terminadas sus **tareas,** *Guadalupe se iba con su pequeño a dormir y yo me quedaba sola, contemplando el sueño de mis hijos. Como la puerta de mi cuarto quedaba siempre abierta, no* **me** *atrevía* a acostarme, temiendo que en cualquier momento pudiera entrar y atacarnos. Y no era posible cerrarla; mi marido llegaba siempre tarde y al no encontrarla abierta habría pensado... Y llegaba bien tarde. Que tenía mucho trabajo, dijo alguna vez. Pienso que otras cosas también lo entretenían...

Una noche estuve despierta hasta cerca de las dos de la mañana, oyéndolo afuera... Cuando desperté, lo vi junto a mi cama, mirándome con su mirada fija, penetrante... **Salté** de la cama y le arrojé la lámpara de gasolina que dejaba encendida toda la noche. No había luz eléctrica en aquel pueblo y no hubiera **soportado** quedarme a oscuras, sabiendo que en cualquier momento... Él **se libró** del **golpe** y salió de la pieza. La lámpara **se estrelló** en el piso de **ladrillo** y la gasolina **se inflamó** rápidamente. De no haber sido por Guadalupe que acudió a mis gritos, **habría ardido** toda la casa.

Mi marido no tenía tiempo para escucharme ni le importaba lo que sucediera en la casa. Sólo hablábamos lo indispensable. Entre nosotros, desde hacía tiempo el afecto y las palabras se habían **agotado.**

Vuelvo a sentirme enferma cuando recuerdo... Guadalupe había salido a la compra y dejó al pequeño Martín dormido en un **cajón** donde lo acostaba durante el día. Fui a verlo varias veces, dormía tranquilo. Era cerca del mediodía. Estaba peinando a mis niños cuando oí el **llanto** del pequeño mezclado con extraños gritos. Cuando llegué al cuarto lo encontré golpeando cruelmente al niño. Aún no sabría explicar cómo le **quité** al pequeño y cómo me lancé contra él con una **tranca** que encontré a la mano, y lo ataqué con toda la furia contenida por tanto tiempo. No sé si llegué a causarle mucho **daño**, pues caí sin sentido. Cuando Guadalupe volvió del mandado, me encontró **desmayada** y a su pequeño lleno de golpes y de **araños** que **sangraban.** El dolor y el coraje que sintió fueron terribles. Afortunadamente el niño no murió y se recuperó pronto.

Temí que Guadalupe se fuera y me dejara sola. Si no lo hizo, fue porque era una mujer noble y valiente que sentía gran afecto por los niños y por mí. Pero ese día nació en ella un odio que **clamaba** venganza.

Cuando conté lo que había pasado a mi marido, le exigí que se lo llevara, **alegando** que podía matar a nuestros niños como trató de hacerlo con el pequeño Martín. "Cada día estás más histérica, es realmente doloroso y deprimente contemplarte así... te he explicado mil *veces que es un ser inofensivo".*

Pensé entonces en **huir** de aquella casa, de mi marido, de él... Pero no tenía dinero y los medios de comunicación eran difíciles. Sin amigos ni parientes a quienes **recurrir**, me sentía tan sola como un **huérfano**.

Mis niños estaban **atemorizados**, ya no querían jugar en el jardín y no se separaban de mi lado. Cuando Guadalupe salía al mercado, **me encerraba** con ellos en mi cuarto.

- Esta situación no puede continuar - le dije un día a Guadalupe.

- Tendremos que hacer algo y pronto - me contestó.

- ¿Pero qué podemos hacer las dos solas?

- Solas, es verdad, pero con un odio...

Sus ojos tenían un **brillo** extraño. Sentí miedo y alegría.

La oportunidad llegó cuando menos la esperábamos. Mi marido partió para la ciudad a arreglar unos negocios. Tardaría en regresar, según me dijo, unos veinte días.

No sé si él **se enteró** de que mi marido **se había marchado**, pero ese día despertó antes de lo acostumbrado y se situó frente a mi cuarto. Guadalupe y su niño durmieron en mi cuarto y por primera vez pude cerrar la puerta.

Guadalupe y yo pasamos casi toda la noche haciendo planes. Los niños dormían tranquilamente. **De cuando en cuando** oíamos que llegaba hasta la puerta del cuarto y la golpeaba con furia...

Al día siguiente dimos de desayunar a los tres niños y, para estar tranquilas y que no nos **estorbaran** en nuestros planes, los encerramos en mi cuarto. Guadalupe y yo teníamos muchas cosas por hacer y tanta **prisa** en realizarlas que no podíamos perder tiempo ni en comer.

Guadalupe **cortó** varias **tablas**, grandes y resistentes, mientras yo buscaba **martillo** y **clavos**. Cuando todo estuvo listo, llegamos sin hacer ruido hasta el cuarto de la esquina. Las **hojas** de la puerta estaban **entornadas**. Conteniendo la **respiración**, bajamos los **pasadores**, después cerramos la puerta con llave y comenzamos a **clavar** las tablas hasta **clausurarla** totalmente. Mientras trabajábamos, **gruesas** gotas de **sudor** nos corrían por la frente. No hizo entonces ruido, parecía que estaba durmiendo profundamente. Cuando todo estuvo terminado, Guadalupe y yo nos abrazamos llorando.

*Los días que siguieron fueron **espantosos**. Vivió muchos días sin aire, sin luz, sin alimento... Al principio golpeaba la puerta, tirándose contra ella, gritaba desesperado, arañaba... Ni Guadalupe ni yo podíamos comer ni dormir, ¡eran terribles los gritos...! A veces pensábamos que mi marido regresaría antes de que hubiera muerto. ¡Si lo encontrara así...! Su resistencia fue mucha, creo que vivió cerca de dos semanas...*

Un día ya no se oyó ningún ruido. Ni un lamento... Sin embargo, esperamos dos días más, antes de abrir el cuarto.

*Cuando mi marido regresó, lo recibimos con la noticia de su muerte **repentina** y desconcertante.*

Glossary

el/la huésped: "host"

reprimir: "to repress"

el parpadeo: "blink"

desdichado/a: "wretched"

inofensivo/a: "harmless"

los quehaceres: "chores"

el pavor: "dread"

gozar: "enjoy"

la pieza: "room"

el mandado: "grocery shopping"

la enredadera: "vine"

florear: "to bloom"

coser: "to sew"

la madreselva: "honeysuckle"

el pensamiento: "pansy"

el gusano: "worm"

la gota: "drop"

la manguera: "hose"

la sombra: "shadow"

la estufa: "stove"

la leña: "firewood"

arrojar: "to throw"

loco/a: "crazy"

perseguir: "to chase"

acechar: "to lurk"

la pesadilla: "nightmare"

el cenador: "gazebo"

la merienda: "afternoon snack"

el rincón: "corner"

cobrar: "to become"

tenebroso/a: "spooky"

la madrugada: "dawn"

las tareas: "household chores"

atreverse: "to dare"

saltar: "to jump"

soportado/a: "to bear"

librarse: "to shake oneself free"

el golpe: "blow"

estrellarse: "to crash"

el ladrillo: "brick"

inflamarse: "to ignite"

arder: "to burn"

agotado/a: "to dry out"

el cajón: "crate"

el llanto: "cry"

la tranca: "bar"

el daño: "damage"

desmayado/a: "passed out"

el araño: "scratch"

sangrar: "to bleed"

clamar: "to cry out"

alegar: "to plead"

huir: "to flee"

recurrir: "to turn to"

huérfano/a: "orphan"

atemorizado/a: "frightened"

encerrarse: "to lock oneself in"

el brillo: "glow"

enterarse: "to find out"

marcharse: "to leave"

de cuando en cuando: "occasionally"

estorbar: "to hinder"

la prisa: "hurry"

cortar: "to cut"

la tabla: "plank"

el martillo: "hammer"

el clavo: "nail"

la hoja: "door jamb"

entornado/a: "ajar"

la respiración: "breathing"

el pasador: "door strike"

clavar: "to nail"

clausurar: "to close"

grueso/a: "thick"

el sudor: "sweat"

espantoso/a: "dreadful"

repentino/a: "sudden"

The time had come for me to board my flight. It was a bittersweet moment, but I knew this wasn't goodbye: Paula and I had become such good friends over the years that we knew we would see each other again on another adventure,

"*Adiós, amiga,*" I said. "*Te extrañaré mucho.*"

"*Yo también, George,*" replied Paula. "*Aprendiste mucho en este último viaje. Te felicito, güey.*"

She gave me a big hug and waved with her left hand as I made my way up the escalator. On the plane, I noticed that the woman sitting next to me was from Guanajuato. Her name was Fiona, and she was pleasantly surprised to see that I knew Spanish.

"*¡No sé qué hubiera hecho si tú no supieras español!*" she said with a shy laugh.

She told me that she was also traveling to Los Angeles but that she didn't know anyone and was afraid that she wouldn't be able to understand anything. At that moment, I had an epiphany: I was meant to be this girl's English tutor! I didn't really know about English grammar as much as Paula knew Spanish grammar, but I was confident in my skills.

Now, I am teaching Fiona English. Everything came full circle, and I am sharing my knowledge with others thanks to Paula's Spanish lessons. *¡Qué emoción!*

Answer Key

1. Lunes: *Nuevas aventuras, nuevas estructuras*

1.
- a. **ante**cámara
- b. **póst**umo
- c. **mono**neuronal
- d. **re**tocar
- e. **des**confiar
- f. **anti**héroe
- g. mar**ear**
- h. ros**áceo**
- i. verdul**ería**

2.

imprimir	impreso	imprimiendo
amar	amado	amando
predecir	predicho	prediciendo
ir	ido	yendo
mentir	mentido	mintiendo
leer	leído	leyendo

3.
- a. *Sigo buscando mi teléfono; no sé dónde está.*
- b. *No te pongas esa camisa, está arrugada.*
- c. *El avión está a punto de despegar.*

    d. *Dieron por concluida la reunión.*

    e. *Hemos pasado horas recorriendo.*

4. Infinitives, participles and gerunds are non-personal forms of a verb because these words carry an action meaning, but they are words that aren't linked to any particular subject. That's why we call them "non-personal forms," because we need to assign this infinitive a subject for us to use it, and that's when this *verboide* becomes an actual verb.

5.

    a. *¡Estoy a punto de tener un nuevo hermanito!*

    b. *Estoy tan triste... El otro día me eché a llorar de la nada.*

    c. *Ando algo adolorida de la espalda.*

    d. *Tengo grabada tu imagen en mis ojos.*

    e. *Llevo 5 años trabajando en esta tienda.*

    f. *Estoy escuchando un álbum de Shakira.*

2. Martes: Si fuera tú...

1.

    a. *Yo **estaba caminando** por la calle cuando escuché un ruido.*

    b. *Marcelo **estaba volviendo** a casa cuando se e4ncontró con Tomás.*

    c. *¡Te **estaba diciendo** que te amaba cuando te quedaste dormido!*

    d. *Ellos **estaban viviendo** en Japón cuando sucedió lo del tsunami.*

2.

    a. *¿**Has probado** la comida polaca? Es muy buena.*

    b. *Yo nunca **he viajado** a las Islas Caimanes.*

    c. *Ellos **han trabajado** en este restaurante desde hace 5 años.*

    d. *Los turistas extranjeros nunca **han visto** un animal tan extraño.*

3.

    a. Wrong. *Si yo **fuese** rico, viajaría por el mundo.*

    b. Right.

    c. Wrong. *Si Juan **hubiese** estudiado para sus exámenes, **habría** aprobado.*

    d. Wrong. *Me **encantaría** conocer Florencia.*

4. False. Type-three conditional sentences express a condition of impossible realization (because they speak of the past, of things we can no longer change).

5.

    a. *Si tuviera más dinero, compraría una casa en la playa.*

    b. *¿Qué habrías estudiado si no hubieras sido médico?*

    c. *Cuando Ana Clara estudia mucho, aprueba todos los exámenes.*

    d. *Si te sientes triste, ¡mira tu programa de televisión favorito!*

3. Miércoles: Lo que nos depara el futuro

1.

    a. *Yo comeré tacos al pastor. / Yo voy a comer tacos al pastor. / Yo habré comido tacos al pastor.*

    b. *¿Conseguirás un nuevo trabajo? / ¿Vas a conseguir un nuevo trabajo? / ¿Habrás conseguido un nuevo trabajo?*

    c. *A María Elena no le gustarán la sorpresa. / A María Elena no le va a gustar la sorpresa. / A María Elene no le habrá gustado la sorpresa.*

2.

    a. *Yo como pollo todos los días.*

    b. *Ella pone la mesa.*

    c. *¿Están organizando el cronograma del festival?*

    d. *Ellos no quieren a su maestra.*

    e. *¿Estuviste buscando a tu perro?*

3.

    a. *Ana le hace la tarea a Nicolás.*

    b. ¿*Puedes llevarle esta carta a tu tía, por favor?*

    c. ¿*Les han ofrecido un café?*

    d. ¡*Debes pagar lo que debes al Estado!*

    e. *Préndele la televisión a tu hermano, por favor.*

4.

    a. *Right.*

    b. Wrong. ¿*Qué **es lo bueno** de tener un perro?*

    c. *Right. Estas vacaciones fueron lo mejor que me pasó en la vida.*

    d. Wrong. ***Lo peor** de la fiesta **fue** que hacía mucho calor y que la música era mala.*

5.

    a. ¿*Qué es lo que quiere esta vez?*

    b. *Te olvidaste de lo que una vez fuimos*

    c. ¿*Es esto lo que quieres hacer de tu vida?*

4. Jueves: La gente anda diciendo...

1.

    a. *Se regalan libros.*

    b. *La gente no sabe nada de matemáticas.*

    c. *Se piensa que el tesoro aún está enterrado debajo del mar.*

    d. *Hay que ir al cine más seguido, ¿no?*

    e. *Dicen que no se puede viajar más a ese pueblo.*

2. False. *La gente*, one of the ways of making impersonal sentences in Spanish, needs a verb in the singular form to be used.

3.

    a. *El perro será corrido por el hombre en la avenida.*

    b. *Las moscas son atrapadas por los sapos cada mañana.*

    c. ¡*Mi sillón de cuero fue destruido por mis gato!*

4. False. The phrase *Yo trabajo como contador* cannot be transformed into the passive voice because the verb *trabajar* is intransitive, which means it cannot affect a direct object.

5.

    a.   *Carla me preguntó si quería comer con ellos.*

    b.   *Martín dijo que el día anterior había visto a su madre sola en el parque.*

    c.   Carlos le ordenó a su hijo que fuera allí.

    d.   Susana exclamó que ojalá lloviera.

5. Viernes: Tomárselo con calma

1.

    a.   *¿Podrías afeitarte antes de conocer a mis padres?*

    b.   *¡Quiero irme de aquí ahora!*

    c.   *Con mis amigas solíamos maquillarnos antes de ir a la escuela.*

    d.   *¿Necesitan ducharse? Pueden hacerlo en mi casa.*

2.

    a.   *¡Bájense de ese árbol, niños!*

    b.   *Quédate aquí, ya vuelvo*

    c.   *Amigos, maquillémonos un poco antes del espectáculo.*

3.

    a.   False. The relative pronoun *quien* is only used to refer to a person, not an object.

    b.   False. The passive voice phrase *Los platos están suciados* is not correct: it should be *Los platos están sucios.*

4.

    a.   Wrong. *Es una mujer cuyo esposo se llama Lorenzo.*

    b.   Right.

    c.   Wrong. *Aquella muchacha de la que me enamoré.*

5.   Translate the following sentences with *estar:*

    a.   *La puerta estaba abierta cuando llegué.*

    b.   *¿Tu dinero está guardado en el banco?*

    c.   *¿Tu hogar está asegurado?*

6. Sábado: Palabras difíciles

1.

   a. *No me pidas que cocine, no **sé** hacerlo.*

   b. ***Se** busca profesora de español.*

   c. *Mi abuela **se** lava el pelo en la peluquería.*

   d. *¡**Sé** obediente y haz lo que te dice tu madre!*

   e. *Compré chocolates en el freeshop y **se** los regalé a una amiga.*

2.

   a. *Este año gané menos dinero **que** el año pasado.*

   b. *Mi hermana, **que** no pudo venir, te manda un cariño.*

   c. *No entiendo por **qué** aún no han llegado los demás.*

   d. *Los pasajeros **que** lleguen tarde no podrán abordar el avión.*

   e. *¡**Qué** casa más bonita!*

3.

   a. Wrong. *Compré mucha salsa picante. **Se** la llevo de regalo a mi padre.*

   b. Wrong. *Ahora entiendo por **qué** dicen que México es tan lindo.*

   c. Right.

   d. Wrong. *En el carro entran **hasta** cuatro pasajeros.*

   e. Right. *Tuve que apurarme para no perder el avión.*

4.

   a. *qué*   4. what

   b. *hasta* 3. not before

   c. *por*   5. for

   d. *sé*   2. know

   e. *que*   1. may

5.

   a. *Vine a México **para** visitar a mi amiga Paula.*

b. *También vine **porque** quería aprender español.*

c. *En su primer viaje, George estuvo en México **por** una semana.*

d. *Siempre que viajo, llevo regalos **para** mi familia.*

e. *Si no te atienden **por** teléfono, prueba hacerlo **por** internet.*

7. Domingo: ¡Nos vemos!

2.

a. False. *Llevábamos entonces cerca de tres años de matrimonio, teníamos dos niños y yo no era feliz* ("We had been married for three years, we had two kids, and I wasn't happy").

b. True. *Vivíamos en un pueblo pequeño, incomunicado y distante de la ciudad* ("We lived in a small town, isolated and far away from the city").

c. False. The story doesn't say what the creature is.

d. True. *Guadalupe arreglaba la casa y salía a comprar el mandado* ("Guadalupe tidied up the house and did the grocerie shopping").

e. True. *Al día siguiente dimos de desayunar a los tres niños* ("The next day we gave the three kids their breakfast").

3.

a. It was a big, dark, and damp room.

b. She liked to sit down in the garden corridors and sew the children's clothes.

c. Martín is Guadalupe's son.

d. Because she has no money, she is isolated, and she has no friends or family to go to.

e. She tells him that it died in a disconcerting and sudden way.

Conclusion

¡Enhorabuena! Congratulations, my friend: you have finally become an official advanced Spanish speaker. It wasn't so hard, was it? All it took was three vacations in Mexico! We hope you have enjoyed this trip to the central region of this wonderful country. Let's look at everything you have learned while traveling with George and Paula, shall we?

El lunes, you focused on prefixes and suffixes to make nouns, adjectives, and verbs. Then, you learned the theory behind the three *verboides* we have in Spanish (infinitive, participle, and gerund) and saw which functions they can have within a sentence. Finally, you saw the different verb paraphrases you can make using these *verboides.*

El martes, you focused on two past tenses of the indicative mood: the *imperfecto progresivo* and the *pretérito perfecto compuesto.* Second, you revised how the *condicional simple* worked and saw another tense called *condicional compuesto.* Then, you remembered what the present subjunctive consisted of, and you learned three past tenses of the subjunctive mood: the *pretérito perfecto,* the *pretérito imperfecto,* and the *pretérito pluscuamperfecto.* Finally, you saw how to make three types of conditional sentences to reflect on the past.

El miércoles, you reviewed the *futuro simple* and the *futuro perifrástico* tenses and saw how you could use the present simple to talk about the future, plus some future time markers. We then focused on the *futuro compuesto tense* and its uses. Second, you learned how the direct object works and which transitive verbs can use this object in different scenarios. Then, you looked at the same thing but in relation to indirect objects and the transitive verbs for said objects. Next, you focused on how *lo* works as a neuter pronoun. Finally, you focused on different constructions that included the neuter pronoun *lo*.

El jueves, you focused on different ways to make impersonal constructions with *se, la gente, uno, hay que* and the third person plural. Next, you learned how to recognize and use the passive voice in different sentences. Finally, you saw what direct and indirect speech is and how verbs are modified.

El viernes, you remembered how reflexive verbs worked and how to use them with modal verbs and in the imperative mood. Then, you saw how to use the word *se* to make passive-voice sentences. You also learned another type of passive-voice sentences – those that require the verb *estar.* Finally, you focused on the morphology and use of relative adverbs and pronouns such as *que, el cual, donde*, etc., and saw how you can pair them with different prepositions when using relative clauses.

El sábado, you saw the differences between *sé* and *se, qué* and *que,* how to use *hasta,* and how *por* and *para* are used in different contexts.

El domingo, you saw some reading comprehension tips, which consisted of focusing on context, purpose, the main message, and text structure, among other things. Then, you learned some writing strategies that involved focusing on the key message and the potential reader, plus making a detailed outline of the text (among other important things.)

If you felt inspired by the Mexican marvels we showed you throughout this book and are planning to book a flight south like George did, we wish you the best of luck!

Muy buena suerte y ojalá disfrutes mucho tu estadía en este hermoso país. ¡Viva México!

If you enjoyed this book, I'd greatly appreciate a review on Amazon because it helps me to create more books that people want. It would mean a lot to hear from you.

To leave a review:
1. Open your camera app.
2. Point your mobile device at the QR code.
3. The review page will appear in your web browser.

Thanks for your support!

Here's another book by Lingo Publishing that you might like

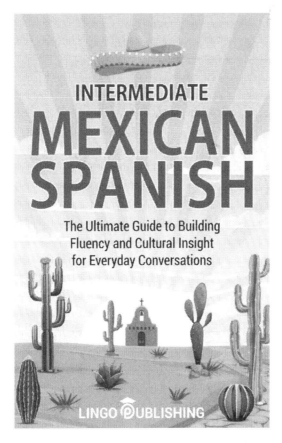

INTERMEDIATE

MEXICAN SPANISH

The Ultimate Guide to Building
Fluency and Cultural Insight
for Everyday Conversations

LINGO PUBLISHING

Free Bonuses from Cecilia Melero

Hi Spanish Learners!

My name is Cecilia Melero, and first off, I want to THANK YOU for reading my book.

Now you have a chance to join my exclusive Spanish language learning email list so you can get the ebooks below for free as well as the potential to get more Spanish books for free! Simply click the link below to join.

P.S. Remember that it's 100% free to join the list.

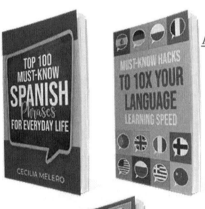

Access your free bonuses here:

https://livetolearn.lpages.co/advanced-mexican-spanish-paperback/

Or, Scan the QR code!

Made in the USA
Las Vegas, NV
28 October 2024

10564410R10077